WORK SMART, NOT HARD

Hard work will never make you richer

Dr. Sriram Ananthan

ABOUT AUTHOR

Canadian Writer, Professor and Entrepreneur, Dr. Sriram Ananthan, has had a burning desire, from as far back as he can remember, to live his life to the fullest and accomplish all of his dreams. Even at a young age, he knew he could grow into a man of great success. Knowing that education would play a huge role in making this dream come true, Dr. Sriram Ananthan went on to earn a Ph.D. in Marketing Management.

Using the knowledge he had gained from his academics, Sriram was able to gain employment working for a bank. Although he excelled in his 9 to 5 job and was able to learn and grow in the area of Marketing, he knew his abilities could be better used guiding other professionals to succeed. Realizing this, he began slowly making his way into the role of Entrepreneur.

Today, and using 13 years of in-depth experience in business development, Sriram serves as a Professor by passion and guides young professionals as they set out on their entrepreneurial path. In doing this, he is able to talk with and motivate them to work hard, gain as much knowledge as they can, and most importantly, always go for their dreams, just as he has.

CONTENTS

INTRODUCTION

The world is brimming with busy people. The individual who's always surging from place to place, always in a hurry, never stopping. They most likely feel that being busy means they're profitable, yet it's not the same. The best people are always accomplishing extraordinary things by apparently doing next to no, and while some would state they're simply fortunate, I'd say that they're amazing at "smart" working; they know unequivocally how to accomplish the most in the shortest possible time.

You know there will be piles of hard work in front of you - in what capacity will you traverse everything? To work viably necessitates that you work smart. There are nevertheless 24 hours in a day; while in transit to turning into an entrepreneur, you'll likewise need to rest, eat, and take care of obligations other than spreadsheets and pitch challenges. Not all things can be outsourced. The road forward will be long and tough. Center, drive and total confidence in your business vision and mission will envelop the center of your being. In any case, realize that the order you call every day to take off of the bed at 5:00 AM, prepared to work hard and smart until 10:00 PM or even later, is the perspiration value speculation that could make your enterprising idea reasonable and maintainable.

To give you some motivation, we should unload the expressions "working smart" and "working hard." The division has resounded through business news sources for a long while, yet lived experience discloses to me that it is a straw man contention. As a general rule, if you need to understand your destinations and objectives, whatever they might be, at that point be set up to work both hard and smart. It has never been either or. It's both.

They are working smart methods organizing and giving rare time and assets to people and activities that convey the ideal results. A few thoughts and exercises are engaging at first look, yet it is possible that they don't can bring the expectations, or you come up short on the assets to oversee it. Your exploration and examination demonstrate that time and cash would be squandered there, so you proceed onward.

For hard workers, hard work is regularly the main departure from the real world, bringing a feeling that all is well with the world and solidness in life. Be that as it may, in actuality, just hard work once in a while prompts the best advancement conceivable in life. You can't just work hard; you likewise need to think and work smart. You can't just be a warrior in life; you likewise need to grow up into a general. Don't just be a hard worker; be both a hard and a smart worker. Presently you know how. The principal thing you can do as a smart worker is to execute the thoughts you preferred the most into your regular daily existence right away.

CHAPTER ONE

Working Hard vs. Working Smart

Working hard is an abused misnomer. Creating great work does not always compare to producing extended periods, but instead is a successful utilization of resources.

Using pointless time or vitality to achieve a goal is a wasteful use of resources. A compelling individual must realize how to successfully explore the workday, deciding which projects are most critical and designating adequate resources to achieve them. Even though working hard may deliver quality work, the quality and amount are probably going to endure except if you are additionally working "brilliant."

Conventional thoughts of hard work incorporate extended periods and physically debilitating work. Even though a fantastic work ethic is essential for success, it isn't adequate. Connecting the estimation of work to the time spent doing it is incomprehensible since mechanical advancements have so definitely changed the way we work. Undertakings that used to take days or weeks can now be cultivated in hours or even minutes. Plus, it is unreasonable to imagine that the old ways of doing things are unrivaled only because they took additional time.

To work "brilliant," you should wipe out diversions since they cause lost core interest. A viable way to do this is to work on a single thing at a time and allocate it a specific deadline every day. By starting with a given end, you are less inclined to stray from your track, and you can quantify your advancement as you move forward. Putting off exercises that can be tended to at some other point is a keen move. You can always return to them after you complete the current assignments. This will enable you to hone your concentration.

Individuals who work smarter experience less pressure, have more leisure time and accomplish more. They don't waste their vitality on irrelevant issues. They realize that a sound system connected reliably yields the best results, both subjectively and quantitatively. They additionally comprehend that the way to success is expanded efficiency without consuming unnecessary effort. A craving for quantifiable results fills their venturesome mentalities, and those results turn into the litmus test for their success.

Working smarter is comparable on a basic level to adaptability. Organizations that need to build versatility go for expanding benefits while additionally expanding deals. They additionally adjust when specific resources are added to the blend. An individual who endeavors to work smarter can achieve more prominent productivity and quality of yield by concentrating on the best utilization of resources. For each situation, the goal is to improve net gains by upgrading resources. If achieved, the two situations present an open door for great development, benefit, and redistribution of valuable resources.

Recovering the workday starts with one acknowledgment: you can do it. Giving the duty to another person or reasoning that daily exercises are outside one's ability to control sends even the most encouraging individual into a descending spiral. Rather than assuming you can't practice any authority over the parameters of your day-to-day undertakings, apply a few and see what occurs. You will find that even little shifts in effort yield quantifiable results, and you can use them to build momentum.

The best individuals hold onto this standard as disruptors. They change the way they consider work and how to create quality results productively. They don't execute using out-of-date standards. What they can be sure of is that the best way to enhance a procedure is to accomplish something different. That "different thing" depends to a great extent on what they are attempting to achieve. Regardless of what the goal is, a keen individual must endeavor to work smarter, instead of harder, to abstain from wasting valuable resources and making do with inadequate results that bargain believability, dishearten joint effort, and disappoint opportunity.

Decide on the Overall Objectives

It is difficult to realize how to work smarter if you are unclear on precisely what you have to achieve. What are your clear-cut objectives—specifically, the all-encompassing goal—and how might working smarter develop it? Clarify your objectives first and after that, make relevant inquiries that outline them further. Who are the pertinent partners? What makes a difference most to them and how do these variables impact your work? Do hours and area influence your capacity to execute viably? What are the business legislative issues and strategies?

After you have a strong thought of what you are attempting to achieve, examine current practices to perceive how they are helping or ruining your advancement. Note where you can make upgrades. For instance, you might confound longer working hours with being progressively gainful. Longer hours, in any case, don't compare to a superior result. They are not one and the same. Updating your procedures might mean achieving quality over the amount of yield.

What's more, you additionally may need to investigate the conditions you are working under. The workplace condition might negatively affect your efforts. Examine your calendar and vicinity to others to identify any diversions. Every one of these components can impact your general objectives. Understanding the lay of the land can enable you to choose how to explore the objectives best and to achieve your goals utilizing the best methodologies.

Evaluate the Rigor of Work

If you have eight hours every day to finish your work, you will utilize your time differently than somebody with a 14-hour window to consume. Furthermore, your work cadence will differ depending upon whether you are doing mental or physical work. One may rely upon motivation and the capacity to produce a bright idea and great contentions. The other may require physical quality and stamina.

"Thoroughness" may change based upon the season. Such is the situation for bookkeepers, particularly amid assessment season. Another way meticulousness may change is at certain periods of a project. You may have a significant push toward the start or the end, yet experience smooth cruising amid the rest of the work year. Comprehending what is required to total the subtleties of your work at every crossroads successfully can augment success.

Set Deadlines

If you need to be proficient, your work requires enforceable deadlines. Be sensible, however, and realize that your deadline can be difficult to meet without sincere effort. One way to approach this is to make both delicate (inner) and hard (outer) deadlines. The delicate deadline is generally optimistic, yet it likewise can give extra audit time before presenting a final, timely item to an outsider. The hard deadline is generally unbending and will direct the project's direction.

You may even need to put the project on an all-encompassing timetable or, contingent upon what is in question, speed it up and renegotiate the expectations. In either case, it is best to match up results with deadlines and separate the expectations after some time to ensure they are sensible and that the work is delivered well in the first go-round. Time and effort are squandered when work must be revamped due to errors. Keep in mind that huge or complex sections may require additional time and joint effort to sensibly and skillfully push through in the time apportioned.

Deal with the Workflow

After you have set your deadlines, you have to piece the work into portions. Most projects can't be finished in one sitting. They should be separated into smaller, progressively sensible pieces or even designated to other colleagues. Some portion of this procedure essentially includes understanding your workforce, pinpointing the specialists, and knowing how much time everyone needs to produce their segment if pieces must be designated. If you are exclusively mindful, ensure you give yourself abundant time to work through each piece of a project completely. Set aside the opportunity to survey your duties against project requests. Examine best-case and most pessimistic scenario situations to make an arrangement in case things don't turn out the way you figured they would. Decide the ideal way to continue, and after that, move forward deliberately.

Execute

When you have made a course of action, the time has come to execute it. To begin with, imagine the goal and afterward, survey the techniques you have created to perceive how each piece fits together. If the project requires the aggregate effort of a group, have a meeting and brief them on the subsequent stages. If a performance effort, you can survey the arrangement and the means determined to deliver the ideal results. Next, make a detailed system. You will need to test these highlights to ensure everything will work fine when the time comes to move forward.

Now is the ideal time to find any hiccups and to address them before they impact the last work item. When you successfully execute segments of the underlying stage, you can build momentum for the more unpredictable ones. Make sure to gauge results and use what you learn and apply it to future situations.

> # We Don't Get Paid For **Hard Work,** We Get Paid for Smart Thinking
>
> - Thach Nguyen

How to Work Smarter, Not Harder

DON'T DIVE RIGHT IN

The vast majority of us have distorted perspectives on how we invest our energy. "If you don't see it on paper gazing at you in the face, you won't realize that you invest excessive energy in Facebook, or that you have similar people interfering with all of your time, posing similar inquiries."

Keep an energy log for seven days. Record what you do, how long it takes you, and who is intruding on you and what they need. "The greatest time-management mistake people make is not realizing how much time they squander. When you break it down, you see what's happening." Also, you'll have an excellent informational collection to figure out how you can shift your time utilization, limit intrusions, and become familiar with a couple of key exercises.

LET SOMEONE ELSE DO IT

To be more successful, you must request help and enrol people who are better at specific tasks and capacities than you are. That requires taking a hard look at your strengths and having the modesty to concede there are a few areas in which you're more gifted than others. You're likely investing more energy than is vital on the things you're not good at. When you can designate those tasks, you free up time to take every necessary step you're best at, which you're most likely going to do quicker and appreciate more.

WORK WHEN YOU FEEL LIKE IT

It might appear as though working smarter means front-stacking your day, so you accomplish more sooner. You are overlooking your ultrafine mood: the 90-to 120-minute example found in our sleep and waking hours. By taking more breaks and cutting up your day into 90-minute segments, you profit by the times of focus you usually have, which can enable you to accomplish more. Focusing on your vitality cycles is basic to working smarter. When you're feeling focused and fiery, you will accomplish more work in a shorter timeframe. "Many individuals are good at high fixation work toward the beginning of the day. Along these lines, if you can, construct your day so the principal thing you work on is the most effective." If you're not a morning person, shift that counsel to when you feel best to take care of business.

READ THE MANUAL

How often have you read the guidelines that accompanied your new telephone, tablet, or another gadget? What amount of time do you invest looking into hacks and energy-sparing measures for the stages you use? If you're like most people, you jump right in and try to figure it out yourself, and you may never learn the real power of the technology you use. Investing time in reading the guidance manual and getting prepared can yield numerous long stretches of return on the venture. Macros, alternate ways, and other time-savers may not be quickly apparent, but they can simplify your work.

BE MORE BUREAUCRATIC

Huge associations don't appear the best model for time-sharing. However, one thing the people regularly do well is systematizing. Some exceed expectations at looking at tasks that need to be done for the organization to capacity and actualize the most time, cost, and vitality productive methods for doing as such. Procedure improvement has turned into an entire industry as more experts endeavour to make tasks effectively repeatable with less time and effort while looking after quality. Take a look at the tasks you perform on a regular basis and how you can create a more proficient method for completing them. Are you sitting around idly, booking numerous arrangements consistently? Take a look at mechanizing that work with a planning application. Are you dealing with a venture with numerous donors and variant control issues? Take a look at how you can create a system of catching input and guaranteeing everybody has the most current data, maybe with a cloud-based collaboration system.

LAY OFF THE JUNK FOOD

What you do outside the workplace affects your capacity to focus. If you're tired and feeling awful because you're not getting enough sleep, proper sustenance, or exercise, that will reflect in your effectiveness and efficiency. The Centres for Disease Control considers inadequate sleep a general medical issue that costs the U.S. up to $411 billion every year in lost profitability.

STARE AT A PHOTO

Consider the reason you need to work smarter and not harder. Do you need more time for yourself to do the things you want to do? Are you simply feeling worn out? Do you need more time to be with friends and family? Whatever the reason, put a photo or gathering of pictures that represent those reasons somewhere you can see them often. This will help keep you on track when you're lingering, investing excessive energy in online social networking, or generally undermining your efforts to complete your work in less time.

Ways for Boosting Your Work Performance

1. Use a timer

I have seen that a standout amongst the ideal approaches to improve my focus while doing PC-related work is to work with a timer.

With a timer, you can make "mini-deadlines," and you'll be constrained to complete however much work is reasonable amid this time square.

I will in general work in 50-minute lumps, so I set the timer, work on my tasks and after that enjoy a little reprieve.

Only turn the timer on and endeavour to achieve however much as can reasonably be expected.

2. Have a task list

There are a few people who like to have paper-based task lists. However, I pursue a tech approach.

Planning a task list shouldn't scare you. All that is required is 10 minutes of your time before you head to sleep (or toward the finish of your work day).

Amid that time, scribble down no less than three essential tasks that you'd like to accomplish the following day. At that point - and if the timetable grants - add some smaller tasks to your list as well.

You will have a blend of tasks that move your venture further while dealing with the smaller tasks.

Having a list gives you a plan to follow. As opposed to just "drifting around" amid your work day, give your day an unmistakable course and work on the tasks that should be accomplished.

3. What are your 20% tasks?

You know those important tasks you ought to focus on? I like to call them 20% tasks.

The term 20% task originates from the 80/20 idea; decide which tasks get 80% of the outcomes when focusing on 20% of the issues. That 20% of tasks are the ones who take your undertakings forward and help you achieve your objectives quicker.

Pick your 20% tasks when you plan your task list for the following day and give them a higher need in your task list.

4. Frogs are very decent (when you complete them)

In this specific circumstance, frogs are the tasks that you'll likely linger on. Since you realize you'll put those off, why not assault those sorts of tasks as quickly as time permits?

When you get the hardest task(s) off your list rapidly, you have more opportunity to focus on the other stuff. If you figure out how to get the "frog" task done as the first thing of the day, your day will be a lot lighter since the most challenging work is finished.

5. Saying "no" isn't impolite

Over and over again, we feel constrained to state "yes" to a request by another person.

When somebody requests that you accomplish something, you can deny their request (in any case, you should help somebody on account of a crisis).

Simply try to assess the request first and after that state "no" speedily, yet delicately, if the request doesn't fit into your timetable.

6. Know the tasks that permit distraction

Trust that a few tasks permit distraction superior to other people.
For example, if you are directing web journal remarks, composing basic answers to messages or doing whatever doesn't require quite a bit of your focus, you can focus on those tasks regardless of whether there is some distraction around.

Make a point to exploit this data when you plan the task list for the day. You may have times when you need quiet. However, specific tasks permit distraction better, and you don't have to keep the workroom entryway shut.

This is uplifting news, mainly for the individuals who don't have a devoted workspace at home.

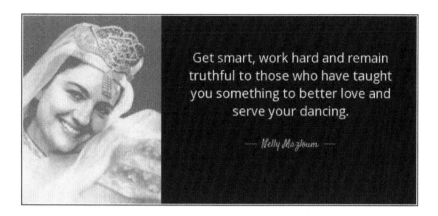

Get smart, work hard and remain truthful to those who have taught you something to better love and serve your dancing.

— Nelly Mazloum —

7. Focus on one task at a time

Continue working on one task, and once you have achieved your daily objective, proceed onward to the following task. In any case, attempt to abstain from working on one task and changing to another before it is complete.

To effectively complete a single task, use these tips:

Break the task into smaller pieces.

Make a plan for your task (use the Super Wednesday Method).

Use a timer if necessary.

Shut/calm down all the additional distractions (email customer, texting, telephone).

Shut out time on your timetable only for the task.

Take little breaks (as it were, don't simply sit for quite a long time on your PC).

One extra advantage of this methodology is that you'll undoubtedly complete the tasks right the first time since you can concentrate on them appropriately.

8. Set the desires right

Tell others how your business works.

For example, you could do the following:

Tell others how regularly/how rapidly you react to messages.

Let them know when you return calls.

Mention how frequently you distribute content on your blog.

Let them know when you are accessible on Skype.

Communicate what your working hours are and when you are accessible for your family (when working at home).

In this way, you "train" others in how you work. When others know these rules, they don't anticipate that you should accomplish something that you are not going to do.

There is additionally less space for clashes as everybody has a reasonable comprehension of how you work.

9. Catch everything (a diversion list)

Over and over again, we are occupied by considerations, ideas, and tasks that fly into our psyche while we are doing our work. So as opposed to giving contemplations a chance to pull us farther from the vital work, catch everything into a simple diversion list.

This is only a bit of paper where you scribble down any ideas or contemplations worth recalling while they happen.

At that point, after the workday is nearly completed, you process this list and do one of the following:

A) Take responsibility for the task right away (if it's a speedy one).

B) Schedule it on your task list for a later date.

C) Dump it. Sometimes, the idea doesn't sound that energizing any longer and it's best to release it (if it's a smart thought, it'll in all likelihood return to you later).

10. Drink water

Drinking water has numerous medical advantages. Research has additionally discovered that drinking water has efficiency in improving advantages also.

In an investigation led by the University of East London, they found that drinking water improves your mind execution by 14%.

So, quit drinking extreme measures of espresso and drink more water.

11. Imitate the schedules of others

Suppose it takes you 60 minutes to compose a report. Then again, your associate or online mate can deal with a similar task in a fraction of the time.

Why not solicit him/her about their method for getting things done and afterward apply his/her practices to your work? Like this, you could spare time on your task and complete it faster.

Maybe you could even "share any useful info" now and then, making sense of how another individual completes a specific task, and you could gain from one another.

12. Make inquiries

Try not to stall out with something you don't understand.

Continue making inquiries to understand the issues you have. For example, when I'm gaining some new useful knowledge, and I don't exactly get the idea, I make inquiries like:

Why?

How?

What?

Would you be capable of providing me with a precedent?

Try not to abandon yourself contemplating open issues excessively without anyone else. Move beyond the detours faster by making inquiries.

13. Leave a task, and later return to it

Sometimes, I face a barrier in my work and experience issues. Regardless of how much I endeavour to discover an answer, I'm simply hitting my head against the wall.

The best procedure (notwithstanding requesting help) is to leave, accomplish something different and afterward return.

Often, I get an answer when I'm working out. My subconscious mind is working out of sight and gives me the arrangement when I have run out of hope.

If you have a hard time pushing ahead with your work, step away from it for some time and return to it later on. This will no doubt accelerate taking care of the issue and completing your work.

14. Get up earlier

If you pursue profitability web journals or books, you have presumably caught wind of turning into an early riser and its points of interest (you accomplish more, you possess more energy for yourself).

If you choose to end up one, there are two specific viewpoints that you ought to concentrate on: understanding how much sleep you genuinely need and after that, choosing to hit the hay earlier.

Sadly, I disregarded these viewpoints when I turned into an early riser a few years prior. When I was waking up early, I was inconsistent with my sleep, making my work harder than what it had been.

So first, choose the measure of sleep you need.

For example, I'm as of now waking up without a morning timer and recording my sleeping propensities into a spreadsheet (when I head to sleep, when I get up, the amount I rested).

After accumulating some data on my sleep (over 30 days), it became simpler to re-implement the early-rising propensity. When I know how much sleep I need, it winds up simpler to alter my bedtime.

Second, don't make such a large number of enormous changes without a moment's delay.

If you go to bed one hour earlier, do the modifications a little bit at a time. For example, you could choose to head to sleep 5 minutes earlier this week and after that, another 5 minutes the following week. In the long run, you will hit your objective.

In this way, waking up earlier becomes less demanding.

15. Remember the last task you worked on before your vacation

Sometimes, you must take a break from work. In any case, do you realize which task you should begin working on when you return to work?

This is the thing that precisely transpired: when I returned to work from an excursion, I didn't have any idea of the task I was working on. I squandered a great deal of time making sense of the stuff that I should do.

Instead of falling into this yourself, "bookmark" your work. In other words, leave a note to yourself (for instance, make a report on your work area), depicting the statuses of the most recent tasks you worked on.

Along these lines, you get up-to-speed a lot faster as opposed to contemplating for quite a long time about what you should do.

16. Be responsible

It's an entirely different ball game to guarantee something to be conveyed for another person (your manager, associate, venture individuals) as opposed to conceding to a due date you made for yourself.

When you consider yourself responsible towards others, you feel strained to complete the work promptly, as guaranteed.

It's easy to skirt the deadlines you set with yourself, yet it's a lot harder to do this when other people are involved.

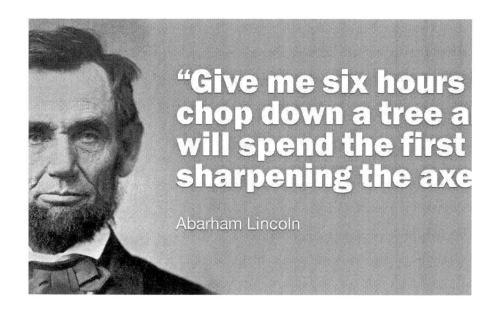

"Give me six hours chop down a tree a will spend the first sharpening the axe

Abarham Lincoln

Ways Small Business Owners Are Working Smarter, Not Harder

1. Build a solid team.

It sounds like an undeniable solution, yet some business owners think it's difficult to hand over the reins. If you fall into that class, try it anyway. Having the correct team on board can help your business thrive — and it can help you feel progressively good venturing without end.

Select the best people to work with. Make beyond any doubt you've plotted the positions you have to fill, and play a functioning role in the contracting procedure to guarantee you like and trust the people you hire.

It's a two-way road. When you build your team to its most astounding potential, your business grows. When your business grows, you can employ more staff. In the year paving the way to our study, 92% of small business owners either kept up or expanded their staff.

2. Utilize the best tools.

Need to be increasingly portable and make your business progressively productive? Putting innovation solutions vigorously is a quick method to do business — and to carry on with your life. Innovation can support you and your staff to complete the work quicker in a less demanding way. Sign on remotely to watch your business and to meet with your teams.

Try "no meeting Fridays." While it's decent to get together with your employees, there's undeniable value in keeping time open to get activities to the end goal, or if nothing else, to the subsequent stage. Days put aside for no meetings can be an important tool, regardless of whether you're working nearby or remotely.

3. Ability to endure hardship.

We've seen small business owner optimism keep on growing since 2013. What's behind it?

Business owners have taken some extreme exercises from past market downturns — 69% have surplus capital on hand. Of those with excess, 35% are putting something aside for future growth, and 19% express the financial emergency instructed them to put something aside for a stormy day. They're prepared for anything and situated to grow.

A fundamental role in the economy

Your role as a business owner is important — to your locale and to the people you utilize. Small business owners utilize 48%** of American workers. They likewise produce multiple times a greater number of licenses per worker than large patenting firms***.

That is the reason it's fundamentally critical to work smarter — not harder — and to set solutions into a movement that assists you in keeping up a work-life balance. The development and energy that originates from small business owners can't be matched. It's infectious. At the point when small business owners are feeling better, they can move the whole economy in the correct way.

CHAPTER TWO

Working Smart and Hard Is the Secret Why Some People Are Poor and Others Are Rich

For the vast majority of people, life isn't a bed of roses. We all need to work hard to achieve success in our occupations, our businesses or even in our relationships. Regardless of working hard, we find that we can't achieve much success and the inviting counsel given to us is to work smart and not hard. There is not a viable alternative for hard work in whatever activity we engage with; however, working smart and hard is positively the ideal way to go about as we continue looking for greatness and success.

1. Working smart implies that for any activity, business or otherwise, there must be a plan. You should initially be clear

about what your goal is and work towards accomplishing that goal. Success is seldom able to be achieved without a legitimate plan. Your very own plan will enable you to achieve your goal.

2. Productivity assumes an exceptional job in the success of a business. Actualizing alternate ways and progressively proficient ways of doing your everyday tasks is a smart way to do your work and expand productivity.

3. Although performing various tasks is a suitable methodology, the vast majority of people think it's difficult to do an excessive number of tasks. Completing one thing at a time proficiently without committing errors and working hard will be increasingly painful.

4. Concentrate on the essential tasks or the tasks that will bring you better returns. This does not imply you are going to disregard the less vital ones.

5. The propensity to be a stickler is lamentably one of the concealed disasters that hinder the success of people who work hard. Desist from being a perfectionist, work smart and hard. All other minor things will fall into place.

6. Act smart and gain rapidly from the mistakes you have committed and from the errors of others. You need not to re-invent the wheel. Simply do what other smart people have done.

·7. Staying up to date with the most recent improvements in innovation in your general vicinity of activity is a normal way of working smart. Utilize software programs, devices, spreadsheets, and online networking to assist you with working hard and proficiently.

8. Identify people who are frequently connected with working smart. They work smarter and but harder, and to the amazement of the others, they discover time to relax and take an interest in other exercises as well. Get assistance from them. Request help. Some of them are extremely happy to help.

9. Delegate a portion of the lesser vital routine work to others and concentrate on the more critical and challenging tasks. This will vastly expand your yield.

10. Working smart and hard can be distressing at times. Enjoy a reprieve at whatever point you feel drained or depleted. Mingle and relax with your companions in the evenings. This will give you the necessary boost and enthusiasm to start another day's work.

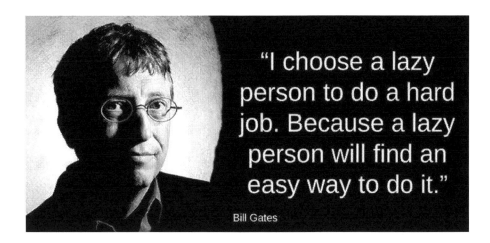

"I choose a lazy person to do a hard job. Because a lazy person will find an easy way to do it."

Bill Gates

The 5 Hidden Clues to a Successful Online Business

1. Marketing

This one needs to go first since you could have the best product on the planet; however, if nobody knows about it, you won't profit. I'm additionally incorporating market research in this section because so regularly, people discover a product they like and after that, they attempt to market it. This is the incorrect way and not how to start a successful online business. You need to do market research to perceive what people need; at that point, make a product to satisfy that specialty. You need to learn and ace the full range of marketing methods out there and watch what the pioneers are doing and copy them.

2. Proven Sales Funnel

When you get people intrigued, you need to send them down a way that will lead to a sale. This is the place you can use the intensity of a proven sales funnel, which is already made for you, so you should point people to the start and afterward observe them fly out the opposite end as a client.

3. Great Content and Delivery

At the point when people have bought your product and touched base on your site, you need to deliver on what you have guaranteed. Indeed, you need to give them undeniably more than they were expecting, such as a free reward or a free course. This is amazing because you have already taken their money, so any additional things you give them builds up colossal affinity and believability. This will help you acquire numerous referrals and your business will boom.

4. Timing

This section is regularly neglected; however, I propose it is very critical and runs hand in hand with your market research. You need to get people right now who have money to spend and are ready to submit. A decent separation here would be Google and Facebook marketing. On account of Google, you are timing your pitch at the point someone types in an inquiry question, so they are effectively searching for something and presumably ready to buy. With Facebook, you are focusing on people who like something on their profile yet aren't presently looking for it; this requires an altogether unique methodology. Right timing will genuinely enable you to draw nearer to that successful online business you are searching for.

5. Track, Evaluate and Improve

The more significant part of the 97% of online businesses that don't succeed fall flat on account of the absence of tracking. From time to time they accomplish something right, yet when they endeavor to reproduce, they have no clue how they did it. In case you seek after the maxim, "If you can't track it, don't do it," you will incredibly build your odds of having a successful online business.

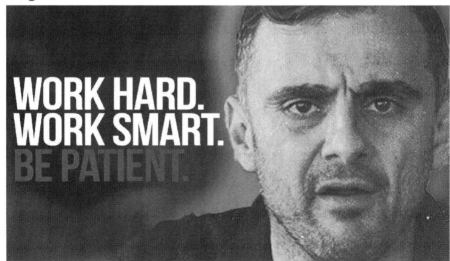

Tips on How to Run a Fruitful Online Business

It isn't such a troublesome assignment to run an online business, but to run a successful online business can be difficult. A large number of people have their very own internet business. A large number of them don't have any fortunes whatsoever. Do you need to be successful when running your very own online business? Here are a few tips you can follow:

1. Before managing to run a successful online business, you will need the required information. Make sure to pick an industry you are familiar with. Along these lines, you will establish beyond any doubt that you realize where to start, and how to manage the issues as they emerge. Typically, you can run a successful online business whether you have past involvements or not. You need to recognize what you're doing before starting. This will guarantee some background information on the industry rather than indiscriminately starting your business.

2. You need to sort out your action from the earliest starting point. The most prosperous online businesses are those that have a prevalent marketing and business plan set up from the start. This will enable you to adhere to your project as the time passes by with the goal that you won't get lost. It is quite hard to be successful when you don't know where you are going. A business plan will enable you to decide and set up how you

need your company to advance, and a marketing plan will direct you on the most proficient method to extend your company. Those two characteristics are synonymous with a successful online business.

3. In case you encounter issues, don't hesitate to request help. Numerous business owners, as a rule, maintain a strategic distance from approaching other people for help since they would prefer not to have their pride harmed. This is something you ought to manage before you even begin. It is an inconceivability to know everything about your industry, so there will be times when you should make a few inquiries. Rather than thinking about this as a terrible thing, why not view it as a way of creating new business contacts and companions? If you encounter a specific issue you can't fathom, you should contact an IT company promptly. You need to comprehend and acknowledge that there is nothing incorrect in doing this. All things considered, if you don't make inquiries, you will never learn, and you might keep down your company.

4. Try not to attempt to reproduce the wheel. Following a settled On-line Marketing Plan, you can take an easy route to your Internet success. In any case, you need to be mindful not to embrace unsuccessful plans.

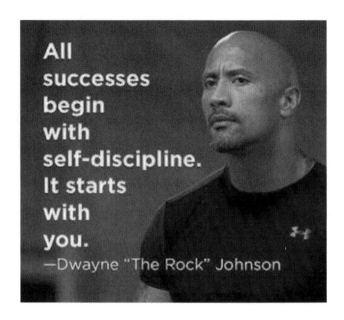

All successes begin with self-discipline. It starts with you.
—Dwayne "The Rock" Johnson

How to Run a Successful Online Business

Online businesses are much more marketable than the neighborhood ones since they can draw in clients from all parts of the world as long as they are dynamic internet users. What does it take to maintain a fruitful business online? This is most likely one of your questions if you need to set up an online business.

Proficient Website

An all-around optimized website is a final device that empowers you to set up an online business. Whatever the business plan is, it doesn't make a difference. A website is a crucial prerequisite. How expertly your website is created decides the number of offers you make.

An optimized website ensures that your business does not pass up the first page rankings of these search engines. Your website ought to appear among the significant page search results. This ensures your website gets a tremendous amount of traffic to boost the business volume. Continuously let an expert website engineer and creator set it up for you. There is no space for negligible missteps if you need to succeed online.

The Right Business Idea

The elements of picking a nearby business idea are the same as an online one. You need to choose a business idea that is feasible and beneficial—one that can withstand even the harshest of financial circumstances. You need a business idea that is as powerful as the internet market requests. It is best not to set up an online business that will fall even before its first birthday celebration. Before receiving an online business plan, it is essential to complete foundation research on the different businesses that are now offering the same administrations as yours after which you can strategize on the best way to profit by their inadequacies. This ensures the online clients can be persuaded that your business is the one with the correct arrangement.

Realize Your Target Market

Some products are just usable by clients of a specific age while others are usable by anybody. For example, if you need to move digital products online, there is hugely no age limit to who can or can't buy the product. In any case, running eBooks with grown-up substance must be acquired by more seasoned internet users. It is essential to distinguish your target market and work towards altering your online business to suit their requests.

Online Marketing Is Key

A business should be publicized or marketed for it to pick up the original presentation it needs to flourish. Aside from search engines, by what other method will a potential customer realize that your online business is moving what the individual needs? You need to put a great deal of time and cash in marketing your business. Different promoting channels can be sought after to yield the ideal marketing results. Email marketing and automated assistants are a portion of the usually utilized marketing strategies.

Customer Relations

You should realize how to relate to your clients and customers. There is no alternate route about it. A fulfilled customer will presumably return with a companion! This is how your online business will be fruitful. Make beyond any doubt that your business offers after-deal administrations, like a guarantee on harmed products.

Convincingly, an online business, much the same as some other endeavor, requires an inspirational frame of mind, a strong will, diligent work and assurance to succeed. These are close-to-home characteristics that will incredibly support the achievement of your online business.

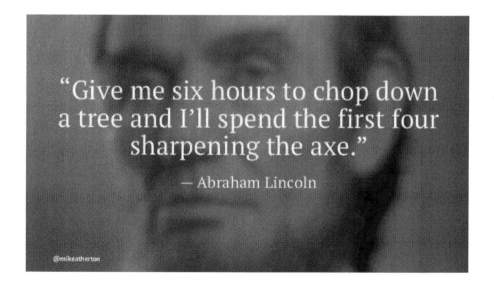

"Give me six hours to chop down a tree and I'll spend the first four sharpening the axe."

— Abraham Lincoln

@mikeatherton

CHAPTER THREE

Proven and Easy-to-Start Online Business Ideas That Make Money

I SACRIFICE.
I WORK HARD.
I WORK SMART.
I AM A PROFESSIONAL.
I AM BUILDING MY EMPIRE.
I AM THE MASTER OF MY DESTINY.
I AM AN

ENTREPRENEUR.

Opportunities come but don't wait. Here is the most recent online money-making opportunities you should do to make the most of current opportunities!

Profiting online isn't new anymore, yet many are uninformed of the different ways you can benefit online.

1. Start a YouTube Channel

Starting a YouTube channel is the most straightforward method for making money online and needs positively no startup venture.

YouTube gets an astounding 5 billion perspectives every day, which demonstrates its capacity on the web. There's no uncertainty how much money people are making on the internet using this platform. One man named Felix Kjellberg, the owner of PewDiePie, earned 12 million dollars in 2015 by running a single YouTube channel.

Making money on YouTube is one of the most straightforward online money-making openings that you can discover. This is fundamental because the platform considers people with essential PC information to leverage their innovative capacities to produce content that can pull in watchers and supporters.

With expanding followership, your YouTube channel is able to be monetized. Your acquiring potential indeed won't be resolved exclusively by the number of supporters and perspectives you have, yet also by the dimension of commitment you create, the niche you give content to, and the revenue channels you investigate.

Release us through the absolute most prominent YouTube niches that are profoundly worthwhile...

1. Video blogs

Video blogs or vlogging includes routinely recording and distributing videos of your everyday life. This can be a straightforward approach to make YouTube content since you can communicate yourself unedited and interface with your adherents on close-to-home grounds.

Trust me, a ton of YouTubers profit from vlogging about their families, school, ventures, wellness sessions, picnics, and so forth. People have stopped their employment and taken on vlogging full time, mainly because it is anything but awkward to start and has an exceptionally high winning potential.

2. Tech Videos

We watch a lot of technology videos, given the distinctive gear that are turning out quickly and how educational they can be, mainly when the distributor is all around grounded in the tech space.

Nowadays, it isn't merely me. A large number of people go on YouTube to watch surveys about the most recent cell phone or find out about a phone they intend to purchase.

If you're a techy individual, tech videos are unquestionably the niche for you. You can get some top-of-the-line gadgets from companies that need you to advance their gear by demonstrating how it functions. This would procure you believability and huge followership as well as swell your pocket.

3. Instructional Exercises

Regardless of whether it is cooking or DIY projects like sewing, carpentry, makeup application, auto maintenance, teaching techy stuff like web composition, and so on, there are dependable people who need to figure out how to do things by watching videos, and you could make money off them by giving the required content.

4. Item Reviews

I'm one of those people who like to watch a video on a thing that I'm considering acquiring to perceive how it functioned for another person. Being a product reviewer can get you free things from companies who require their items to be put out there for limited-time purposes and some significant money to tail it.

5. Comedy

"All work and no fun makes Jack a dull kid" goes the well-known axiom. No one jumps at the chance to be a Jack, and this is the reason numerous people like to participate in some fun activities like watching comedy videos on YouTube.

Realize how to get animated comedy plays, or you can for the most part effectively influence people to unwind and giggle. Distributing comedy videos may be your entryway to YouTube money-making opportunities.

You can bear witness to the way humorists are living substantially off the high group of onlookers they get from their original videos, mainly because they have monetized their channels.

So, you see, there are many niches you can wander into with regards to making money off YouTube. The rundown is unending.

Luckily for understudies who go to our digital marketing course, we not only open them to many profitable YouTube niches and revenue channels, but we additionally show them how they can leverage these chances to start their mogul venture off YouTube.

YouTube promotions are by a wide margin the most effortless approach to procuring money on YouTube. As of late, anybody could use YouTube to make money.

Yet, that all changed as of late when Google reported they would raise the measures required to have promotions appear on your channel.

Presently, you should be a piece of the YouTube Partner Program (YPP) and meet specific criteria so you can start profiting from promotions. These include:

Having at least 4,000 watch hours

Anchoring at least 1,000 endorsers over the most recent year

Frightening, right? There's no compelling reason to stress. Our digital marketing course causes our understudies to become familiar with the best systems to expand their endorsers from zero to shocking numbers and furthermore, to supply video content that will get fans stuck to your channel for quite a long time.

This is a standout amongst the best-privileged insights that YouTubers are utilizing to make money nowadays.

This online money-making opportunity is best for people who love to make videos, talk in front of a camera, shoot comedy clips and movies, and so forth.

2. Start a Blog

Being a blogger is one of the most straightforward approaches to making money from home. Unlike numerous other jobs that require a lot of time, blogging is entirely different because you don't need to work from an office space; you can blog right from your comfort zone in your home.

Fortunately, blogging comes with multiple revenue streams, such as the following:

Selling e-books on your blog

Selling online courses

Offering paid freelance services

Making money from affiliate marketing

Show Google promotions on your blog (advertise products and brands)

Start an e-commerce store (sell products on your blog)

You can likewise create a paid private gathering and sell premium content like tutorials and products.

Blogging enables you to work whenever you like, and it doesn't take the whole day. It's flexible.

But you have to take note that nothing great comes easy, so blogging takes time for you to start profiting. Your best method of starting is to design a blog and develop your audience, utilizing a few strategies in this post.

If you have a day job, don't quit. You can create your blog and work on a part-time basis.

3. Begin Affiliate Marketing

This one is a kind of execution-based marketing in which organizations remunerate a specific level of commission for every item purchased by clients who were lured by your affiliate marketing exertion.

4. Create Niche Websites

A niche website is a concentrated on one specific topic that shares all data applicable to the topic that is both valuable and intriguing for the intended interest group.

It tends to be any little scale web property that makes money. By and large, a niche website ought to have these attributes:

It has a low number of substance pages (Usually 20 or less).

It is barely engaged around a specific topic or group of onlookers.

It depends on a solitary wellspring of salary.

It gets traffic from one place (as a rule, from a Google search).

For example, you can create a website around the niche of land. The objective can be to plan property visits by proposing mortgage holders. You can likewise create a website that is based on paid music.

After choosing the niche you wish to enter, you should now create content adjusted to that niche and direct people to the website — the more traffic you have on your site, the more your adaptation openings increment.

Some niche website adaptation openings include the following:

You can show Google advertisements on your niche website

You can likewise show your own advertisements on your website. For example, if you run a land niche website with high traffic, you can motivate real estate agents to publicize their administrations and home contributions on your website.

On the other hand, you can make money from composing supporting posts and item audits for organizations. This works best for people who run high traffic innovation websites.

Many individuals move exceptional items like digital books, formats, online classes (paid video instructional exercises), webcasts, and so on.

Affiliate marketing is your surest bet. You can easily advertise your custom affiliate connects to platforms like Amazon and start to make money by advancing the connections in blog entries on your niche website.

5. Distribute a Kindle eBook

Do you have excellent writing skills? Are you a storyteller and can assemble a substantial following of people who would pay money to your accounts?

If you are searching to adopt this skill, you ought to consider distributing ebooks on the web.

What the large distributing houses do with large workplaces for editors, writers, managerial staff... and afterward, huge printing squeezes... at that point, dissemination focuses on getting their books out to bookstores around the nation... all to ideally get books in the hands of readers.

... all of which you can do on the PC you have at present.

If that is not a huge business open door for writers and distributors, I don't know what is.

Distributing an ebook on Kindle is one of these basic, rewarding plans; however, it is an uncommon approach to produce steady, easy revenue on the web.

Did you realize that Amazon is the most significant opponent to Google than some other search engine like Yahoo and Bing?

An ever-increasing number of customers attempt to search for an item on Amazon than other customary search engines.

At the point when people need the top-to-bottom data on a specific topic, they go and search for eBooks on Amazon to get valuable suggested books.

Mainly, you can use the blasting solicitation for these eBooks and create a steady automated revenue source.

Here's the secret...

To start with, what is an Ebook?

Ebooks are books that are conveyed, downloaded and once in a while, read on the web.

You can think of them yourself (or utilize writers). You can create your ebooks from numerous sources. What's more, pretty much any subject can be secured like travel guides, how-to manuals, puzzles, sci-fi, self-improvement, innovation, etc.

Additionally, you won't need to depend on a supervisor or distributer to reveal to you whether a book will be distributed. What's more, you won't need to rely on a bookstore to put your book on its racks. You're in complete control of the whole procedure.

Indeed, you're going to deal with everything yourself, including marketing and moving. Furthermore, that implies you get the chance to keep every one of the benefits. Astonishing right?

When you know how to do this, composing ebooks on Amazon requires some choice skills to distinguish the niches that will benefit you. Using digital marketing skills and systems like catchphrase research and web-based life marketing will help get your books sold.

6. Create a Membership Site

A membership site is a membership website with a particular substance made accessible to a specific number of joined clients.

This kind of website gives a place to enrolled individuals to interface with each other, and there is a monthly expense to join.

This online money-making opportunity is best for people who like to collaborate, guide and lead a network.

7. Sell Websites on Flippa

People fabricate websites, not for their utilization but instead to be purchased, and this is one of the most recent online money influencing openings we have.

In this way, Flippa is primarily a place where you can sell and purchase instant websites.

On the whole, you should almost certainly create and structure sellable websites for a beginner. This is the entire substance of the platform. Our digital marketing course understudies figure out how to create shocking websites without any preparation, utilizing instruments like WordPress and topics that are eye-catching.

In case you're willing to commit some capital, a moderate measure of time and a lot of undergarments, flipping on Flippa can net you some genuine money. The platform has seen more than $140 million in deals since its 2009 dispatch, making it an excellent platform for you to start to profit from.

At the point when your website is seeing a stable measure of traffic, commitment and money related potential, it's an ideal opportunity to sell it on Flippa.

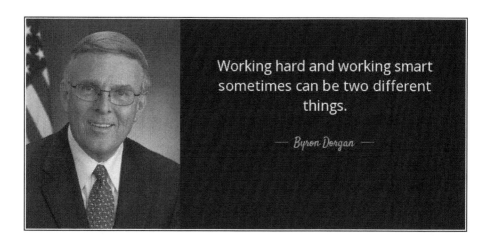

Working hard and working smart sometimes can be two different things.

— Byron Dorgan —

8. Sell Services on Fiverr

Fiverr is where people offer undertakings, service, and products for as low as 5 dollars.

Fiverr gets around 5 million monthly visits, and your point ought to be to leverage on the regularly developing interests of Fiverr gigs and make predictable, secure revenue doing what you love to do.

You need to concentrate on offering outstanding service to receive great reviews. With that under control, you'll get new and repeat clients from selling your services.

To begin with, when you enroll in our digital marketing course, you'll figure out how to design websites, create lovely illustrations, have an eye for incredible website topics, and fabricate your online profile to allow people to look for your services on the web.

9. Do Facebook Marketing

Facebook has over 1.9 billion active monthly clients. With the broad scope of highlights, Facebook is a standout amongst the best places to achieve your market target crowd.

Facebook is a social platform where organizations go to advertise their products and services. Thus, numerous entrepreneurs don't genuinely realize how to showcase their products on Facebook and other web-based social networking websites.

Without much stated, you can leverage your digital aptitude from our digital marketing course to give Facebook marketing services to forthcoming customers.

10. Do Email Marketing

Email marketing is another type of offshoot marketing where you utilize your email rundown of blog supporters to advance a specific product. With email marketing, you can profit online without leaving your home.

This online money-making opportunity is best for people who love to talk, compose, clarify and influence.

Email marketing has its strategies and methods. It accompanies being a talented sales rep who can compose marketing content that would not be considered nasty and can sell their products or those of different organizations.

Sadly, numerous organizations lose a great deal of money enlisting on the web advertisers that guarantee to realize how to do email marketing yet they end up having few open rates (people who open your emails) and an exceptionally irrelevant transformation (rate of people paying for your product or service from your emails).

11. Start a Podcast

A podcast is a computerized sound record made accessible on the web for downloading to a PC or other convenient media player, ordinarily accessible as an arrangement, new portions of which can be gotten by endorsers naturally.

You can move these podcasts as opposed to giving them out for nothing. Guarantee they are convincing, intelligent and unique.

We gain a ton of traffic, commitment, and even cash from discharging podcasts that are genuinely beneficial. Since it is only sound, people won't get the chance to see your face.

12. Build Software

Software improvement is the procedure of PC programming, recording, testing, and bug settling engaged with making and keeping up applications and frameworks bringing about a software product. It requires the learning of any programming dialect.

13. Compose Articles on Authority Websites

Numerous authority websites are searching for new content and ideas to extend their client base and augment benefits.

Thus, they require new people with ideas who can carry out the responsibility for them.

Numerous websites will pay you to compose content for them. This encourages them to catch new ideas and points that generally would have never been discovered by their content group.

14. Become a Graphic Designer

Correspondence is profoundly influential when business targets meet visual style in like manner. Let's face it: graphic structure is utilized to influence its intended interest group to think about the plan before the brand.

Graphic design is a standout amongst the essential parts of business since graphics is something that grabs our eye and pulls us towards products and brands.

Quality graphics incorporate the brand's picture with customer's eyes, they make a robust, constructive impact on people.

Because of the ascent of the web and innovation, new businesses are starting every day, and that why the requirement for eye-catching graphics has turned out to be critical to numerous businesses.

You can use this chance to change your fortune.

As a graphic designer, a large portion of your jobs will incorporate websites, logos, print headers, banners and product interfaces.

15. Turn into a Video Editor

If you like making videos and altering them, but you would prefer not to start a YouTube channel, you can utilize your abilities to encourage different businesses. Because of the enormous fame of YouTube and Facebook videos, businesses around the globe require experts who can alter their videos.

You can start by searching for gigs on freelancing websites. At first, you will work with irregular clients, yet not long after, you will have a couple of standard clients offering you enough work to cover your time. You would then be able to develop your business to start an office or contract different specialists to assist.

Don't know how to make or alter videos? Try not to stress; there are a lot of online assets offering free and paid instructional exercises and courses. You can contribute some time to get familiar with the essential aptitudes and start working immediately.

16. Turn into a Storyteller

Storytellers give voice to video makers, movie producers, and other advanced content makers. Many YouTube channels are actively searching for people to describe videos. Some essential voice preparing can help you effectively start a productive vocation.

You will require a decent quality mic (we suggest Samson Mic or Rhode Podcaster) and sound account software to record your voice-overs. You would then be able to send the sound recording to the client so they can utilize it in their video.

You can secure positions on freelancing websites, and very rapidly construct a constant flow of clients.

17. Offer Technical Support

Do you like assisting people at tech gatherings? If you do, you can investigate chances to get paid for that. Many online businesses are actively searching for specialized help suppliers to encourage their customers.

Fundamentally, you will need to acquaint yourself with the product and start answering questions. Numerous organizations utilize live talk or a help ticketing framework to answer customer questions. Often, these jobs are remote, which implies you can work from your own home.

18. Turn into a Lead Generation Expert

Lead generation specialists enable businesses to discover potential new customers or leads. They do this by utilizing proficient apparatuses like OptinMonster to catch leads or lift change rates.

19. Gmail Extensions

Present-day businesses depend on email to complete their work. There are dozens of opportunities to build Gmail extensions that automate parts of a professional's workflow to spare them time and money.

20. Drone Videography

Improvement in aviation technology has made it less demanding than any other time to get an automaton up and flying over a beautiful scene or building. Businesses and private land owners are asking for more automaton videographers to come in and serve their specialists and home designers.

21. Chatbot Builder for FAQs

Companies squander dozens of hours responding to help inquiries from their clients. Help them mechanize this procedure by utilizing a simple, fitting and playful chatbot!

22. Drop Shipping

You can start a web-based business without holding any stock. This is known as drop shipping. It accompanies truly generally safe and vast amounts of upside if you can overwhelm the right niche.

23. Make a Course

If you know an industry or assignment truly well, you can without much of a stretch make and move an online course that shows people another aptitude. You need to put the assets in advance of building up the real class.

24. Run Social Media Accounts

Start running social media accounts for various companies. Publicize your capacity to drive deals and increment ROI by utilizing the range of different social channels.

25. Turn into a Web Influencer

It is each child's fantasy these days to end up a big web name. What's more, in light of current circumstances, being popular on the web gives you huge power and impact over your group of onlookers, which can be adopted at scale. Here is a quick guide I built to turn you into an influencer.

26. Affiliate Marketing

Affiliate marketing is an organization that you (the blogger or marketer) have with an online retailer. They pay you a commission for each referral deal you send to them. Note: if you're on the opposite end and need affiliate marketing, I suggest you find a decent company. I'm a significant enthusiast of Robert Glazer at Acceleration Partners. They've treated me continuously right.

27. Event Planning and Promoting

Eateries, clubs, and other physical scenes regularly battle to get clients in the entryway. Utilizing your capacity as a marketer, you can help guide traffic to these areas.

28. Real Estate Investing

In any market, there are open doors for purchasing and pitching land to make a benefit. With a touch of capital, you can start going out on a limb on your advantages and making long-haul interests in private and business land.

29. Ghostwriting

You can transform your capacity to compose well and rapidly into a genuine business if you find the right customers. For whatever length of time that you give predictable and quality substance, after some time, your business will undoubtedly develop.

30. Content Translation

Being conversant in another dialect is incredibly important to people who need their websites deciphered. Set up a simple website and you can start charging for "interpretation as an administration" for websites, records, and introductions.

31. Flipping Websites

Utilizing Flippa, or some other online business marketplace, you can purchase and move ventures, areas, and websites. With the right eye, you can find incredible arrangements on promising thoughts and turn them for a benefit with only a little interest in the right regions. I for one have possessed the capacity to make a decent substantial pay every year off doing this.

32. Start a Newsletter

Building a newsletter with an active following is an extremely lucrative business opportunity because sponsors will pay serious dollars to get their names before the right crowd. Start with a little niche that you can truly offer some benefit to, and you will see your rundown of supporters develop after some time.

33. Freelance Designer

Figure out how to utilize Photoshop or sketch, and you can start charging customers for your work. As a specialist, you get the opportunity to make your very own hours and direct your movement as your business develops.

34. Personal Trainer

If you like keeping up a healthy lifestyle, being a wellness coach might be an all-around adjusted business. There is dependably a vast supply of people who are hoping to get fit as a fiddle (and willing to pay for it); they need the right individual to push them towards the right bearing.

35. Craigslist Flipping

Craigslist is a gold mine for finding bargains that you can flip for a profit. There are a lot of assets accessible online that can enable you to identify great arrangements from whatever remains of the pack.

36. Stock Investor

Invest your energy and money into turning into an ace at putting resources into the financial exchange. While returns are commonly unstable and loaded with risk, you can rapidly step up your assets by playing the market amusement effectively.

37. Farmers Markets

If you know any farmers in your general vicinity, you can connect with them and offer to move their item at farmers markets. Instead of paying in advance, you can moderate your risk by joining forces with the farmers in return for a commission.

38. Paid Advertising Consulting

Most businesses depend on a type of paid publicizing to drive leads for their business. Become an expert at AdWords or Facebook ads and you can charge clients for managing their ads.

39. Coaching

Whether it is for the ACT/SAT or naturally broad schoolwork, understudies dependably need assistance getting through their classes. Turn this into an asset that truly enables understudies to prevail in the classroom and guardians would love to pay you for the assistance.

40. Outsourced Assistant

Well-paid CEOs do not have the time or energy to worry about many of the administrative tasks that currently come with the job. If you can give rich people their time back, they will gladly remunerate suitably. Make a point to stamp on your logbook times to work.

41. Become a Reviewer

Trust it or not, you can profit as a "proficient reviewer," otherwise known as somebody who surveys items by distributing his/her thoughts about them online. It will require some investment to increase some area expert, yet sooner or later, you can come to be an idea chief in your space.

42. Life Coaching

Turning into a life mentor is as simple as finding which past encounters you can use to offer some benefit to other people. Regardless of whether it is giving actionable strategies or general advice, you can almost certainly find a niche as a life mentor/tutor.

43. Build Websites

There are a lot of companies and experts out there who truly need a website to speak to them online; however, they don't have the right stuff to do as such. They are more than willing to pay for a quality website that will better show their image picture.

44. Article Writing

If you are a good writer, you can earn money by writing articles for people with websites.

Numerous website owners realize they have to keep their websites current and up to date, yet they don't have the time to create new content constantly. On account of that, they enlist individuals who can compose for their benefit.

With the end goal for you to end up a content writer, here are a few things you can do:

Post a profile on freelancing sites, for example, Elance.com, Guru.com, andOdesk.com. Portray your interests and your dimensions of expertise.

- Look for writing jobs on similar freelancing sites and apply for them.

- Google writer job openings.

Ask the owners of websites that you effectively like if they are searching for writers.

What amount would I be able to make from writing?

Content writing jobs pay somewhere in the range of $1 to $100+ dependent on the length of the article and your expertise. If you're already an expert on the topic you're writing about, you can often charge a premium.

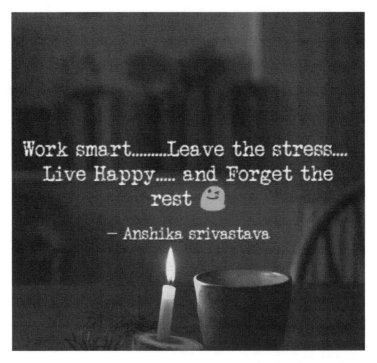

Work smart.........Leave the stress....
Live Happy...... and Forget the
rest 😜

— Anshika srivastava

Tips to Running a Successful Online Business

Whatever sort of business you choose to work from your home is your choice. However, there are a few things you need to do to help you in being active. While considerations and any expectations of a higher hope for everyday life ring a bell for distributing of individuals who choose to begin their very own online home business, they frequently don't recollect that it is by the day's end a business.

Dealing with an online home-based business frequently gives individuals the unfortunate mix-up that they could manage each territory of the businesses' tasks; however, while there are a few angles in which they are accountable, customers would likewise have a contribution on a considerable lot of other capacities.

1 - The primary things you need to maintain a home business effectively is you should have a calendar. It may be anything but difficult to stay up late, watch a movie, and after that more than once press the snooze button the following morning. However, with regards to managing customers via phone, you genuinely don't need them to believe that their morning call woke you up from a deep rest. Keep in mind that having a lot of extra time may be exceptionally engaging and taking the intermittent rest amid the day may be alluring, but attempt to keep ordinary working hours; this is vital to any online home business.

2 - Try to guarantee that your office is utilized for office-related exercises; in addition to the fact that you would get a tax reduction for cutting out an extraordinary space that would be used just for work, you would likewise have the sentiment of preparation for work when you venture into that room in the morning. Similarly, when the workday is done, and you leave your office, you ought to have the sentiment of achieving home. You would need to fend off loved one's diversions from the office similarly as you ought to likewise keep work diversions from whatever is left of the home.

Having an expert methodology in all business actuates when in your online home office would insubordinately help your picture as an online home business owner. You can't stand to have a different telephone line for the business, endeavor to answer the phone in a business-like way amid working hours.

3 - Promotion and marketing is essential to your business; it doesn't make a difference if the business is online or disconnected. The odds are that you don't have a sign hanging at the front entryway of your home that tells passers-by that you are open for business. The primary way anyone will realize that you are open for business is through advancement, promoting and showcasing.

You need your customers to explore and get all the fundamental information on your products; it should fill in as a business flyer that incorporates information about your encounters, your business, and your products. Having contact information on the first page is vital to getting more business and customers; you ought to likewise have a frame accessible for guests to answer questions or to send demands for information.

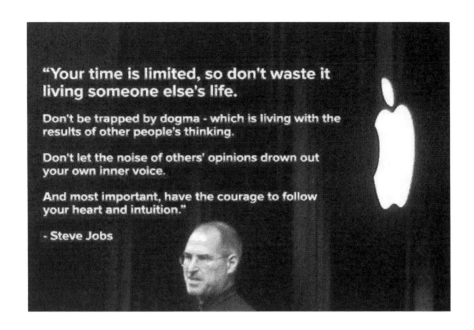

Reasons Offline Business Must Have an Online Presence

1. Improving Your Company Image

This by itself ought to be sufficient motivation to start a new website and begin selling online. Without a website, blog, or online presence, imminent clients can't start to consider how genuine you are about business. Today, organizations and businesses set up fruitful online appearances.

If you don't have an online appearance (and a professional one to boot), you can't anticipate that your prospects should consider you important and you will lose business to contenders who do have a viable online presence.

2. 24-Hour Service

While some drive-thru eateries, markets, and corner stores oversee 24-hour service, it is outlandish for general businesses. That is, without the internet. A key advantage to having an online business website is that your clients and prospects can find out about your items and spot orders at any time—day or night on standard business days or holidays. Envision what being open 3-4 times longer could do for your business.

Regardless of whether you have a customary disconnected service type business, you can create leads and requests while you are closed and follow up with those prospects and customers once you open the following day.

3. Better Customer Support

The internet enables you to respond to questions, give online courses, and tackle customer issues—all without taking any of your time. Make a video, an item spec sheet or a FAQ area, and you can guide clients to that information for a considerable length of time. In addition to the fact that it saves you time, you'll be giving better service. Your clients and prospects are searching for specific information, for example,

Before they settle on a buying decision.

To take care of an issue with a current buy.

Inquiring about choices before settling on a buying decision.

With an online appearance, you can give them the information they are searching for and exactly when they are searching for it. This implies fewer telephone calls with specific inquiries and more sales.

4. Extremely Low Start-up Costs

You can start an online business with low startup costs. You have no buildings to build, no vehicles to purchase and scarcely any staff to hire. Construct your website and start moving. If you are already selling offline, then this can be very smooth. You keep moving similar items that you know and have a good supply of. Putting your company online gives you another wellspring of customers.

You can redistribute a great deal of the specific stuff and even things, for example, online networking promoting.

While you could burn through countless dollars building up the best website and internet business arrangement a significant number of your rivals will do it on a shoestring. A good website can be structured essentially and for almost no cash.

Utilizing a free stage like a self-facilitated WordPress blog and an expert quality premium topic ($70 - $200), you can assemble an expert site independent from anyone else. Some web facilitating organizations offer free site-building instruments.

With a good WordPress template, it is feasible for you to plan your very own site and do it with (nearly) no coding.

To begin on a shoestring budget, hope to pay anywhere from a couple hundred dollars to a couple thousand. The essential costs incorporate web facilitating, WordPress topic, area name, and email showcasing autoresponder service. When everything is set up, it can keep running on autopilot.

5. The Internet Was Made for Business

The excellence of the internet is that your imminent client(s) can truly be only a single click away from your online store. Through the internet, you are able to teach, educate and take care of clients' issues. You can acknowledge orders and installments and get them to your inbox.

You'll want to find out about new viable and reasonable approaches to direct people to your website; the more people who discover you online, the more leads and sales you'll make.

6. Live/Work from Anywhere

Taking your business online enables you to have area opportunity so you can live and work from anyplace you need; you do not need to adhere to a physical location.

For whatever length of time that you have a stable internet connection, you can live virtually any place while you direct your online business.

With a couple of individual cases, the internet lessens your need to "be" someplace. Live where you need to, and let your business adjust to your lifestyle rather than the other way around. There are some important exemptions, similar to exterior decorators, specialists and home painters who must be in a specific area to play out their work.

Obviously, as engaging as this all sounds, having an online business isn't for everybody. There are numerous reasons you ought not to start an online business and keep your day work or conventional business.

7. Diminish Operation Costs

Only one single errand can have a significant effect on cost funds. For instance, accepting orders online decreases the requirement for customer service staff. With exhaustive sales and item information online, you'll get orders and installments using email or into your database. Staff numbers can be diminished, hence office space and related office costs.

A great sales video, sales letter, or online course introduction can supplant a full-time sales individual.

Making use of different online service suppliers, you are able to take all parts of your business online, for example, buying, charging, order satisfaction and delivery. Different capacities can incorporate pre-emptive customer service, for example, responding to client questions using a FAQ segment or a customer discussion.

8. Focus on the Global Market

With your physical business, you are restricted to the measure of people who can visit you at some random time, not to mention discover you. With a good website, you can genuinely have thousands, even many thousands (even millions) of people visiting your online store on the double. Envision the potential for your company, if you could uncover your items and services to a conceivably vast number of intrigued people.

Having the capacity to have many guests and having them are two different things. The accomplishment of an online business relies upon the same thing from any disconnected business: advertising. Figure out how to increase blog traffic. Content showcasing is an incredible method to increase traffic to your site/online store. Online life can be a ground-breaking and reasonable (free) approach to drive qualified prospects to your site. I'd be delinquent if I didn't say that acing the specialty of copywriting is a standout amongst the essential aptitudes to figure out how to increase sales.

9. Increase Company Responsiveness

The internet enables you to deliver your proposition, buy order, order affirmation rapidly—by and large in a split second—to your clients. Online stores will process orders and affirm them to the client. In the past, purchase orders were called in, sent or dropped off. Contingent upon the workload of the sales staff, it could have taken hours or even days to process the order. With a sufficient online store application, you can automatically track inventory, sales numbers, outstanding orders - everything.

Quicker reaction time implies more joyful clients and less managerial work for you.

These are the absolute most dominant reasons you should take your disconnected business online. With every one of the advantages of having an online business numerous people are moving their conventional businesses and propelling online businesses for the time, area, and money related opportunity it offers.

Work Smart - Not Hard - to Succeed with a Home Business

If you have worked for a large company before, the possibility that you are the only person in your company is a test for some people starting a home business. Out of the blue, you are in charge of everything - emptying the paper bins to installing software to balancing the books.

Before you begin feeling overpowered, recall that the trap with a home-based business is to work smartly. One reason you chose to work from home was to have greater adaptability and self-sufficiency, so tried that. Working keen will likewise give you more opportunity to do what truly should be done - in your work and individual life. Think about these tips for working more astute - not harder.

Prioritize

Each night, make a list of what you have to do the following day. Organize the list, putting the most vital and critical things at the top. At the bottom of the list ought to be the things you can easily procrastinate on for a day or two without having any real effect on your business.

Be Realistic and Ruthless

When setting up your plan for the day, be realistic about what you can accomplish in a day. Be ruthless as well, and cut out whatever isn't fundamental. Your need is to get your business ready for action and to make cash - everything else can pause.

Automate Wherever Conceivable

If there are any business processes you can computerize without breaking the monetary allowance, do so. Bulk emails to your database, database management, and other client relationship management tasks can be outsourced to a company that spends significant time in these tasks. It doesn't need to cost a fortune and could spare you cash as well.

Outsource When You Have To

There are a few tasks that you won't oversee yourself. Regardless of whether it's balancing the books, introducing another printer or composing a 500-word article, if you don't have the capacity and it is taking far longer than you might suspect it should, or than you can bear to spend, at that point, it's time to take a look at outsourcing. If the time you are spending endeavoring to adopt new aptitudes is worth more than the cost of getting another person to do it for you (in a fraction of the time), you ought to outsource. You can't do everything, and in actuality, you shouldn't attempt to.

Ask for Help

Frequently, individuals won't approach their companions for help, through pride or a feeling of needing to demonstrate that you can do it all alone. Swallow your pride and request help - especially if your companion is progressively experienced or capable at something you are battling.

Ideally, your home business is keeping you occupied. When you can, give some idea to how you can do things more astute. It might mean updating your PC so you can work quicker, purchasing programming that will help make specific tasks simpler and programmed, or outsourcing to those with the mastery you are deficient. Some portion of your 5-year plan for your home business ought to be to work less, not more!

CHAPTER FOUR

Offline Business Ideas

Nowadays, having an online presence for your business appears to be practically required. In any case, that doesn't imply that every business needs to concentrate on the web. Indeed, there are still a lot of offline open doors for entrepreneurs who aren't tech savvy to consider. Here are 50 offline business thoughts.

Cleaning Service

You can begin a house or office cleaning service where you travel to your clients and utilize local promoting or verbal exchange to construct your business.

Child Care

Child care is another prominent in-home business thought. You can maintain the business out of your own home or go to your clients' homes.

Mortgage Broker

A mortgage broker is an intermediary who brings mortgage borrowers and mortgage lenders together, but does not use its own funds to originate mortgages. A mortgage broker gathers paperwork from a borrower and passes that paperwork along to a mortgage lender for underwriting and approval. The mortgage funds are lent in the name of the mortgage lender, and the mortgage broker collects an origination fee from the lender as compensation for services. A mortgage broker is not to be confused with a mortgage banker, which closes and funds a mortgage with its own funds.

In-home Elderly Care

There's likewise a significant interest for in-home elderly care. You can provide services to customers in your area every day or on a semi-regular basis.

Espresso Cart

With an espresso truck business, you can move your truck to the areas where customers are probably going to assemble, which means you don't even necessarily need a site or other online presence.

Food Truck

Even though it might be helpful to advertise food trucks via web-based networking media platforms, you can set up this kind of business offline and utilize local events to pull in customers.

Gift Shop

It's additionally conceivable to set up a local gift shop with no sort of online business store, insofar as you're in a great location that customers are probably going to visit.

Caterer

You can begin a cooking organization to provide services for events, people and businesses.

Pastry Specialist

You can likewise begin your own business as a pastry specialist, either with your very own bread kitchen storefront or by giving heated merchandise for different enterprises and pastry kitchens in your area.

Plant Specialist

If you're searching for an open-air business thought, you can set up your own planting business and provide services to customers in your locale.

Arranging Service

Moreover, you can offer grass cutting or other finishing services without a site or full online presence.

Pet Cleanup Service

There's likewise a market of pet proprietors searching for businesses to enable them to tidy up their yards.

Home Staging

For configuration arranged entrepreneurs, you can begin a home organizing business where you help local homeowners set up their homes to engage potential purchasers.

Home Painting

You can likewise concentrate on home painting, either inside or outside or both.

Jack of all Trades

If you're exceptional at fixing things around the house, you can likewise begin your own business where you provide general jack of all trade services to customers.

Print Shop

Print shops help clients print anything from signs to shirts. What's more, you can even provide a spot where customers can total their printing and replicating occupations, all from an offline location.

Direct Mail Marketing

If you need to assist businesses with offline promoting, you can begin a direct mail business that centers around written words sent, as our forefathers would have done it.

Gathering Entertainer

For the individuals who are musically disposed or have different abilities like juggling or inflatable chiseling, you can offer your services to customers looking for gathering excitement.

Quaint Little Inn

If you have a sufficiently extensive space, you could set up your quaint little inn where you welcome guests.

Personal Shopper

You could likewise begin your very own shopping business where you run with clients to stores and help them select the best items.

Event Planner

Or on the other hand, you could concentrate on event arranging where you work with clients in person and manage merchants fundamentally via phone.

Errand Service

It's additionally conceivable to set up a general errand running service. You can do things like getting staple goods or wrapping up clothing.

Food Delivery

You can offer food delivery services to customers who need to arrange from restaurants that don't provide conveyance.

Flower Specialist

A flower shop is another excellent offline business opportunity. You can open your very own location and manage customers basically in person.

Ranchers Market Vendor

If you move flowers, plants, food or similar items, you can likewise procure your very own corner at local agriculturists' business sectors and move your merchandise that way.

Adornments Maker

If you make adornments or similar items, you can move them in person at specialty fairs or even discount to local boutiques.

Attire Designer

For the individuals who make a dress, you can likewise concentrate essentially on offering your items discount to local stores as opposed to setting up your online business webpage.

Mentor

It's likewise conceivable to construct a business as a guide. You can concentrate on a specific subject and spotlight on in-person one-on-one sessions.

Canine Walker

If you're interested in beginning a business where you get the chance to spend time with adorable creatures throughout the day, you can offer canine strolling services to people in your neighborhood.

Pet Grooming

You can offer pet prepping services, either in your committed location or as a component of the mobile business.

Mobile Retail Boutique

You can set up a local shop in a trailer or alike and move merchandise at fairs or different events.

Car Wash

You can likewise begin your very own car washing or itemizing business without having an online presence.

Bicycle Repairs

For the individuals who are talented with bicycle repairs, you can create a business around that ability in your carport or a local storefront.

Mobile Phone Repairs

There's additionally a great deal of interest for mobile phone repairs. You can set up a business where people can bring their gadgets with broke screens or different issues.

Cultivating

If you have enough land and the aptitudes to cultivate crops or different kinds of food, you can sell your food items to retailers, restaurants or different businesses.

Corn Maze

There are different choices for those with some land to work with. For example, you can create a corn maze and some correlative attractions and welcome customers to your location.

Christmas Tree Farm

You can likewise develop pine trees on your territory and welcome guests to come to select their very own trees amid the Christmas season.

Visit Guide

If you stay in a city that is quite known with sightseers, you can set up a visit to manage a business where you show guests around.

Security Service

You can likewise begin your security service, giving insurance to businesses or people on an agreement basis.

Craftsman

For aesthetic entrepreneurs, you can create your work of art to move at exhibitions or exceptional events.

Massage Therapy

You can likewise work with clients in person as a masseuse or back rub advisor.

Personal Trainer

You can begin a business as a personal trainer, working with customers at local exercise centers or from your home.

Antique Shop

You can likewise begin your very own antique shop where you move items out of a storefront, antique shopping center or at local events.

Creator

While digital books have increased in notoriety in recent years, you can, in any case, construct a business by composing and distributing real books too.

Speech Specialist

Essayists can likewise construct a business around composing talks on a freelance basis.

Dance Classes

If you're a talented artist, you can offer move classes out of your home or a dance studio.

Music Lessons

Similarly, you can offer music exercises to people hoping to get familiar with a melodic instrument or improve their vocal aptitudes.

Career Counseling

It's likewise conceivable to fabricate a business where you help people discover careers.

Moving Service

If you have a vehicle and some moving supplies, you can offer moving services to local shoppers.

Expense Preparation

You can likewise help people and businesses prepare their duties by meeting with them in person.

Pledge Drive

Pledge drives are additionally in extreme interest in a few areas. You can support businesses and associations fund-raise through events and various crusades on a freelance basis.

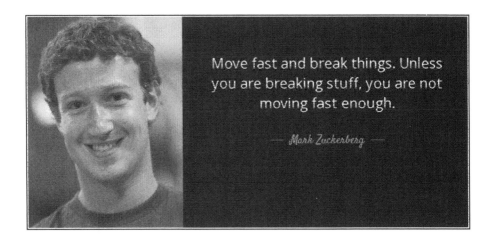

Move fast and break things. Unless you are breaking stuff, you are not moving fast enough.

— Mark Zuckerberg —

Offline Business Skills That Serve You Well Online

You convey a great deal to the table with your offline business skills! Let's look at the gifts your offline business experience brings.

1. You are comfortable asking for what you (or your product) is worth

It's tough to be successful in business if you can't move beyond the "asking for money in exchange for something of value" challenge. If you've had business success, you are OK with this essential skill that makes people squirm.

This will prove to be useful when you are creating, pricing, and offering your products and services online.

2. You know how to find clients and customers

Business success originates from finding buyers for your offers — and you have aced the entire procedure:

Pinpointing your optimal customer

Connecting and creating prospects through offline marketing

Closing sales with a conversation about the value

Serving customers well, so they return for additional products/services

You'll invest heaps of energy searching for the right prospects online as well. The technique you'll use to discover them will be different, yet the overall procedure is the equivalent.

There's an immediate line from offline to online marketing — you'll need to include a couple of skills — more on that in a moment.

3. You know how to create offers people buy

You have mastered the art and science of creating an offer that people need and are happy to pay for. This is no small accomplishment.

It takes guts to make an offer, and you are no more interesting to the sentiment of helplessness that accompanies offering your product or service to the world. You have felt that dread and done it in any case.

The seven new online business skills you'll have to build

You most likely arrived online realizing you have a long way to go.

Shrewd brands today are taking the "omnichannel approach" — joining offline and online endeavors.

(It's occasionally called the "o2o idea" — see that? You simply adapted some extravagant language.)

Some online success stories are notwithstanding moving the other way! They're taking their online success to their offline endeavors.

For you, however, how about we take a look at the seven skills to concentrate on acting first as you develop your offline business success to online business success.

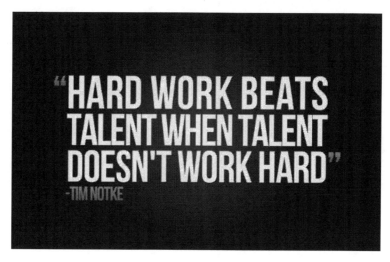

7 New Online Business Skills You Must Have

1. Building a reasonable, drawing in, high-changing over the site

You might be accustomed to running a retail facade or an office. Regardless of whether you have a home office, you realize your condition impacts how people see you.

Duplicate that by 1,000 to understand the significance of your site to your online business!

Stop and think for a minute: online, your site is your business.

2. Gathering an audience

With your online business, you'll use what might be unfamiliar tools like:

Content marketing, where you'll offer supportive, valuable data as blog entries, sound, or video — or a mix of all three.

Internet-based life marketing, where you'll get the message out about what you do on platforms like Facebook, where people as of now gather online.

Visitor appearances on different sites and digital broadcasts, to help spread the news about how you serve your optimal customers.

Online, you should continue thumping the drum of your business, so prospective customers hear and react.

3. Creating opt-in incentives to encourage sign-ups to an email list

As you get the word out about your online offerings, you'll want to gather that audience of prospects in one place where you can communicate with them.

The best spot to assemble your prospects is on an email list.

What's more, the ideal approach to urge people to add their names to your email list is to offer a helpful select in motivator that is so alluring; they're willing to welcome you into their inbox to get it.

When you've fabricated an email list, you'll utilize the following new skill to build incomes.

4. Using email marketing to communicate

An email list will give you a channel you can use to draw in your readers, and serve them up supportive information and resources from time to time.

Email marketing is a minefield. You would prefer not to email again and again — however, it won't work if you don't email frequently enough.

Finding that ideal email marketing balance is one of the problematic tasks another online business proprietor must handle.

5. Building luring online offers

Generally, you don't have the advantage of knowing your online customers personally.

You'll have to utilize "stealth" strategies to understand their requirements and to build products and services that assist their needs.

Here they are, from the most fundamental to the most advanced and complex:

Request that people answer to your email messages. You'll see their answers directly in your inbox.

Answer questions on your blog. Prop the substance discussion up.

Make inquiries and read answers via web-based networking media platforms. Discover what your followers are considering!

It has never been simpler to look in the background of the businesses you go up against. For additional information on the most proficient method to do this, read *Competitor Analysis Tools: 14 Quick Ways to Compare Websites.*

Make an online poll. Make sure to ask some open-ended questions and give respondents a space to reply in their very own words. These words can be mined to compose marketing that quickly reverberates!

Audit your site and social examination to understand actual conduct. Numbers don't lie — cross-check what you hear with hard information to best understand what's occurring in your online business.

6. Creating sales conversations

Online, we don't have administrators remaining by or a beguiling salesperson to shake hands, make another companion, and smooth the path for our prospects to end up customers.

Online, the business discussion is virtual.

Also, it happens one of two different ways: through a "dispatch" or with an "evergreen" offer.

Online dispatches follow a well-known example:

You buckle down for more than a little while to build a list of people who will be intrigued by your forthcoming offer.

In the past, you made your product accessible and you presented accommodating training that gave prospects a look at how their lives or businesses would improve once they had your product or service.

You make your product accessible temporarily — and potentially to a limited number of people.

You offer impetuses for purchasing now.

You "close the entryway" and quit selling the product or service.

Evergreen products come in two flavors:

The on-the-rack product that sits on a shop or store page and can be acquired every minute of every day.

The product that is made accessible to a limited number of people once they've traveled through some sort of pipe, similar to a Facebook advertisement > an online course > a business page.

Trust it or not, you can utilize both of these methods for an individual product or service.

You can make an offer accessible with the evergreen technique that moves prospects through an instructive channel — and consolidate it, so your offers are accessible temporarily with some reward content.

That is an unusual online business skill.

Smart work pays best. Trust it.

— Conor McGregor —

Tips for Becoming a Productivity Superstar

1. Make habits that help productivity

It is usually said that forming a habit takes between 20 – 30 days when done more than once (consistently). This depends on the habit you are attempting to form.

With regards to productivity habits, these are the ones that I have connected in my work:

· Cutting down TV time.

· Disconnect from the web while working (in any event, killing email notifications, texting customers), and turn off your telephone.

· Clean up your work space when you have completed the process of working.

· Let other relatives realize that you are working, so they don't aggravate you.

· Wake up ahead of schedule and work amid the morning hours.

· Create your task list each prior night before heading to sleep.

As you can see, there are a considerable number of things that can be turned into habits. However, you should start working with habit changes step by step, and repeat them often enough so eventually you will be doing them automatically.

You can likewise include your changes and habits to the rundown, with the goal that you can turn out to be much progressively gainful.

2. Have your end goal as a primary concern

Before you even start working, you ought to have your end goal as a primary concern: Why am I working? What am I endeavoring to accomplish? For what reason do I have to get up right on time to work on my business?

When you have the goal plainly characterized (for example, gaining $3,850/month from the items and administrations you are giving or stopping your normal employment before the first of September, 2011) and you remember it constantly, it is less demanding for you to figure designs at a progressively definite dimension (day by day/week by week/month to month).

3. Plan your day and your week

It is important to keep in your mind what you will do the following day and the following week.

On Sundays, I plan the next week's timetable (what I need to achieve), and before hitting the hay each night, I characterize my arrangement for the following day.

My tasks are lined up in light of the end vision. When you have that set (in tip #2), your weekly and daily task records turn out to be a lot simpler to do.

4. Concentrate on one task at once

Numerous worthwhile business openings are thumping at our entryway consistently. We get besieged with messages by different bloggers and web advertisers about the most recent glossy thing.

As enticing as it begins with another venture while you are as yet finishing the past one, you ought to rather complete what you are doing first and afterward move to the following task.

This will guarantee that your task is completed, and that, from that point onward, you will most likely give something else your complete consideration. For instance, if you have your blog dispatch coming soon, complete that first with the goal that you will then be able to continue to different tasks, similar to specialty webpage building.

5. Concentrate on one task at any given moment

Shifting your concentration to a lower level, you should work on one task at any given moment. For instance, if you are composing your blog post, at that point, do that and nothing else.

Checking your Facebook record or associating with others on Twitter while composing your blog post isn't the correct approach.

6. Eat nutritious food all the time

You may not know about this. However, there is a connection between your productivity and what sorts of foods you eat.

You should dispose of unreasonable measures of sugar, awful fat and wheat flour from your eating routine. When I think about these fixings, any cheeseburger feast comes in a split second to my psyche.

There are different foods you may have thought of as of now that are not beneficial for you: pizzas, burritos, most barbecue foods, desserts, candy, white bread, and white pasta.

I could continue forever, yet you get the idea. Nonetheless, I tend to support these standards in my eating routine:

· The less sugar, the better.

· Vegetables, roots, crude nourishment: salads, carrots, tomatoes, seeds.

· Fewer yet better starches: wholegrain bread, wholegrain rice, wholegrain pasta.

· As much natural nourishment as can be allowed.

Before rolling out any extreme improvements to your eating routine, you should check with your doctor about what kinds of foods fit you best. The precedents that I have given are appropriate for me.

7. Get enough sleep

I have discovered that I have to get enough sleep to work well and to increase my productivity.

In the wake of getting 7-8 hours of sleep routinely (this changes for each individual), you will almost certainly concentrate well, recollect things all the more effectively and focus on your tasks.

Sleep is the establishment of your prosperity and productivity.

8. Increase productivity by working out

Exercise to increase your productivity. Even though you may imagine that the time you spend at the gym or on practicing different games is squandered, it is the opposite.

You feel much improved, you fuel your innovativeness, and you are more empowered to work exceptional timeframes.

Have a workout, scrub down after that, and you will feel simply incredible – prepared to assault your tasks!

I enjoy the following activities: going to an exercise center, running, cycling, swimming, and cross-country skiing. You may have different games that you find intriguing.

Consult with your doctor first to comprehend what your present circumstance is and what sports are most appropriate to you.

9. Have a standard timetable – consistently

Build up a calendar for your work. For instance, you may compose your blog post one day, advance it the other, etc.

Any way you choose to structure it, having a calendar is basic. It offers structure to your day with the goal that you will realize when to concentrate on which sort of task. Plus, by making a structure and going through it again and again, you are framing another propensity.

10. Do the most significant thing before anything else in the morning

Make it a habit to get up ahead of schedule and do the most important task you have before anything else. In this way, you will have completed the work should anything surprising happen later, amid the day.

For instance, I get up at 05.30 AM, work on my online business for 45 minutes (important thing #1) and hit the exercise center or swimming pool (important thing #2) before setting off to the workplace.

I realize that regardless of whether something unforeseen happens later amid the day, at any rate, I have accomplished something important to draw me nearer to my goals.

11. Identify the vacant spaces in your schedule

Sometimes, you may have a specific time that is underutilized. Work on your business at that point!

At whatever point I travel; I attempt to exploit travel time by working on the substance for my blog/list or preparation material that I have on my hard-drive.

I make the best utilization of my time – rather than simply viewing the landscape.

12. Make your workspace tidy

The measure of messiness in your workspace influences your productivity. That is the reason it is important to keep your work area spotless and possibly have the basic stuff around your work area when you work. Additionally, it is important to have every one of the things that identify with your work effectively available.

I need to keep my work area as spotless as possible. It just holds a few papers that are identified with my work, 2 screens, a mini-computer and two or three pictures for my delight.

When I quit working, I clean my work area with the goal that my workspace is as welcoming as possible when I return to the workroom. The less stuff there is around my work area, the less distracted I am so I can accomplish more work.

13. Be reliable

Respect others and their timetables by being reliable. If you state you will meet a friend at a particular time, appear as agreed.

However, if you will be late for reasons unknown, let your friend know by sending a text message.

14. Communicate clearly

Attempt to speak as clearly as possible to avoid any misunderstandings. Make sure others can hear you and understand you clearly.

15. Try not to be hesitant to get the phone

In this universe of e-mail and online correspondence, you may need to use some more conventional devices to get the work done quickly.

For example, if you need to discover some data that will help you in your work, take a stab at calling the person directly, if possible.

16. Approach others for help

Regardless of how good you are at what you do, sometimes you are going to need the help of other people.

17. The 2-letter word that will save your day

Say no whenever you feel that you are spreading yourself too thin. If your schedule is already booked, it is going to be booked even more solid because you just allowed an extra task to eat at your time.

Saying no will cut down your commitments and keep you from spreading yourself excessively thin.

18. Document everything

I'm a major enthusiast of documenting everything that is new to me.

For example, there might be a sure way to use a piece of software. If I feel that I have difficulty remembering how to perform a particular task with it later, I will write a step-by-step document. This saves me time because I don't have to spend time remembering how something was supposed to be done.

Another extra benefit of doing this is, if you decide to outsource the task to someone else, you have the guidelines ready for that circumstance.

19. Always be sure, don't guess

I find that valuable time is lost because I didn't double-check something. That is the reason I need to be sure and not guess – on anything.

20. Group as much as you can

When you group, you attempt to complete whatever number tasks as could be expected under the circumstances without a moment's delay. You could write a certain number of blog posts, or handle all your e-mails in one go.

Whatever you do, you will understand that grouping tasks together rather than doing them separately will save you time.

21. Give up on perfection

The best way to destroy your profitability is to keep on tweaking and tweaking your stuff (composing a report, e-book, e-mail to a JV partner, blog post ...) and endeavoring to make it perfect.

Perfection doesn't exist; good is enough. You will continuously be able to improve your stuff at a later date. A lot of tweaking and seeking perfection won't help you.

22. Always use time logs to make your day more productive

Do you know how you consume your time? Is it spent on essential tasks or not?

One way to figure this out is to have a time log. In its simplest structure, it tends to be only a piece of paper with notes about what you did and when. After gathering enough sample information, you would then be able to analyze it and decide how to proceed.

You should record every activity you do amid your day: when you start and when you finish. Then, you can essentially group the tasks into different categories, for example, hobbies, work, TV, internet surfing, etc.

By doing this for at least a week, you will have a good idea of how your time is spent. At long last, when you have done that, you can optimize your schedule, eliminate certain parts that are non-productive, outsource some parts, etc.

23. Keep your home clean

A clean home is a healthy place in which to live. You know where your stuff is, and you don't have to waste time searching for your car keys or other critical things.

You will feel a lot lighter after settling on this decision, and your home will be more rapidly and easily accessible.

24. Always be prepared

Being prepared is yet another way of being more productive. When you are ready, you are prepared for something to happen, and when it does, you will have everything under control. You can remain quiet and handle the circumstance with no problems.

For example, if you are traveling and you don't have access to the internet, you can prepare to do some work that doesn't require internet access (for instance conceptualizing points for blog posts, free reports or e-books or composing your next e-book or blog post).

Being mentally prepared is equally vital. For example, you may be asked to make a little presentation when meeting your customers. However, if you are prepared for the likelihood in advance, it will be a lot easier for you to step in front of an audience than it would be with no mental preparation.

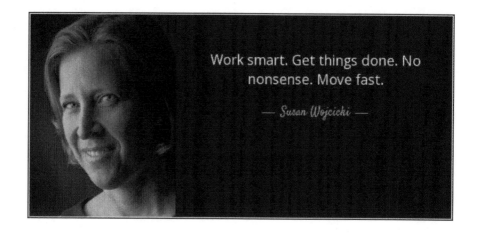

Work smart. Get things done. No nonsense. Move fast.

— *Susan Wojcicki* —

25. Create a mastermind group or go along with one

Gather a cluster of like-minded entrepreneurs (for example, online business owners) and create a mastermind group with them. Then, in every meeting, make yourself accountable for what you need to achieve by the next time you meet.

You will be accountable to yourself and to the rest of the group too. That will make you push your boundaries to meet the deadlines.

26. Hire a coach/mentor

Another way to drive yourself to get more things done is to hire a coach. Like in mastermind groups, you make yourself accountable to a specific person, instead of to a group.

The effect is still potent. You will get more things done than you would without a responsible partner.

Besides, your coach can save you time by giving you the guidelines to concentrate on the essential parts of your business.

27. Outsource your work

You have just a limited amount of time available to you. It is useless to endeavor to do everything without anyone else. Instead, you ought to define the vital parts that require your attention in your business and let the other tasks be taken care of by an aide.

Whether it is redistributing a single task to someone else or procuring a remote helper, you will save time either way. Besides, as a rule, your helper will perform the task a lot faster and better than you.

28. Set deadlines

Rather than spending time endlessly on a project, you should set a deadline.

Setting deadlines for your work makes you work harder to meet them. As an entrepreneur, you will have plenty of other ideas you need to implement, so why spend an infinite measure of time on your present project? The sooner you finish, the faster you can move to your next project.

29. Business first, pleasure second

It is effortless to turn on the TV and undertake that you will watch 5 minutes before getting to work. Before long, you will realize that you watched 30 minutes and that your business was stopping amid that time.

Set your priorities straight by putting business first and pleasure second. You will be more productive, and you won't feel blameworthy when staring at the television (or whatever you will be doing).

Determine to work on your business first, with the goal that you are entitled to do fun stuff afterward.

30. Take massive activity the correct way

When working, endeavor to work as intensively as can be expected under the circumstances. Try not to write only one blog post; write five. Try not to comment on only three blogs; comment on ten blogs. Create seven videos without a moment's delay.

31. Focus on fundamental things

Notwithstanding how many moves you make; you can make a move on the wrong things. This is the reason it is important to focus on the most important parts of your business.

For example, if you see that you are getting a lot of traffic from YouTube rather than social bookmarking sites, you should focus on YouTube as a channel to bring visibility to your online business.

You can follow your traffic sources by utilizing an instrument like Google Analytics to see the measurements. This causes you to choose the correct focus point in this circumstance.

32. Educate yourself with time management books

Sometimes, you will require new ideas for your time management practices. That is the reason you should possess a book on time management to acquire learning regarding the matter.

33. Concentrate a time management system

There is a wide range of time management systems out there; you can discover which one suits you the best by experimentation.

The system you are utilizing does not have to be exceptionally intricate. In its least complex structure, your system could be only a pen and paper and your task list for the following day. Likewise, you will need to have your tasks set in connection to your true objective, so you are endeavoring to achieve your goals, as opposed to handling irregular tasks on your task list.

34. Join an online seminar on time management

Sometimes, you may adopt more on time management by signing up for an online course.

35. Turn into an early riser

You will most likely work focused because there are no distractions to occupy you (if you wake up before your family). When you do your most important tasks of the day before anything else, you won't need to worry over them throughout the day.

Not just utilizing the early morning hours to work on your business, you will likewise have the capacity to practice before going to work.

36. Take power naps

I used to take longer rests – one-hour long ones. I was always drained and sluggish when I woke up.

I once accidentally took a 20-minute rest, and I was stunned how much better I felt a while later! I wasn't worn out or languid any longer – I was prepared for some activity immediately!

By taking a quick snooze, you reload your batteries, and you significantly improve your efficiency. Sometimes, I set a timer for 20 minutes. However, I wake up before it – completely revived!

If you feel tired amid the evening hours, take a power nap to return to business!

37. Take amazing breaks

At whatever point you work (on your PC), take visit breaks. What's more, when taking breaks, you should avoid your PC. Or maybe, you ought to accomplish something different amid your break time.

The breaks are for your efficiency as well as for your inventiveness. Sometimes, another idea may spring up in your mind while taking a break.

38. Complete what you begin

Numerous individuals are anxious to begin accomplishing something; however, they never complete it. What's more, as long as you have a task you haven't completed, you will continue thinking about it.

Endeavor to make the propensity for completing what you begin. Along these lines, you can focus your psyche on progressively important tasks – rather than consuming your vitality on unfinished business.

39. Try not to overstuff your plan for the day

Less is more, and this applies to the number of tasks on your to-do list.

It is anything but challenging to overstuff your task list for a given day – to understand that you are not ready to do everything you arranged. Right at that point, you feel vanquished, because you didn't achieve your daily objectives.

Chop down the most extreme measure of tasks as much as you can. Attempt to have, for example, three tasks on your list; however, make those tasks the important ones. Celebrate completing those three tasks.

Likewise, attempt to have an idea of what your following day will resemble and utilize that data when arranging your task list. If there is something additional to do the day, it's pointless to have ten tasks on your list, when you can only complete two of them.

40. Figure out the profitable pieces of your day

I have understood that there are sure pieces of the day when I feel the most effective. For me, these times are the hours of the morning (06.00 AM – 09.30 AM), evening (01.30 PM – 3.30 PM) and night (7 PM – 9 PM).

I identified these by watching myself and seeing when I completed the most. When I had at last identified these beneficial times, I endeavored to think my work time amid those hours.

41. Utilize a timer to put yourself on efficiency overdrive

The least difficult things can improve your efficiency the most – like a timer, for example.

I suggest utilizing a timer – either on your PC or an outside one around your work area. Alternatively, you can set an alert on your cell phone as well.

42. Reward yourself

You have to work hard on your most basic tasks, yet you should reward yourself too. Even though the request is business first and delights second, joy has its job.

When you compensate yourself, feel qualified for your reward. When you get the reward, know that you have worked well and have pushed your limits to meet the objective (and getting the reward).

The greater the reward, the harder you work for it.

43. Be responsible for your companion or companions

If you don't have the likelihood of joining brains or contract a mentor/guide, you should consider yourself responsible for your life partner or your companions.

This is another way of freely pronouncing what you will do. What's more, when you have proclaimed it openly, it puts weight on you to complete things as guaranteed.

44. Be responsible on your blog, email list, Facebook or Twitter

Your blog can provide you with another way to become accountable. Announce your goals there, so your readers can realize what you are going to do. You can do this by emailing your list or updating information on Twitter too.

Wherever you publish the information, once it's public, it is a lot harder for you not to do what you promised.

45. Go offline when you work

When you work, you work. This implies nothing else ought to be finished amid that time; for example, checking your email or the tweets on Twitter.

You could haul out the fitting of your network, kill email notifications, close the Twitter app or just close down your texting customers also.

Along these lines, you can limit online diversions and focus on the current tasks.

46. Re-appropriate your household chores

To spare time and better focus on your online business, you ought to likewise redistribute different repetitive tasks.

One way to deal with this is to redistribute those household chores that you don't care for doing. Having your home or having your windows cleaned are examples of these tasks.

Whatever the task is, when you redistribute it, you get more opportunity for yourself and your business.

47. Make business ideas when you are offline

Best of all, your brain is working for you while you exercise. This spares your time, since you don't need to set a different meeting to generate new ideas for your ideas. Rather, new and crisp ideas fly into your head while working out. Those ideas can spare your time when you return to work (for example, if you figure out another way to make your working propensities progressively effective).

48. Try not to break the chain

This is an efficiency tip initially made by Jerry Seinfeld. What it implies is that you mark a letter "X" on the divider calendar for every one of those days that you have worked on your venture or task.

When you have worked two or three days, you can see a chain figure develop. If you happen to miss one day and you don't get the chance to draw that "X" on your calendar, your chain is broken.

The more days you have worked in succession (and stamped "X"), the harder it is for you to break the chain. You are putting weight on yourself to continue working without fail.

49. Set updates on your electronic calendar

Setting updates on your electronic calendar is a certain way of helping yourself to remember the things you need to do sometime in the future.

The central idea of having an update is that, rather than endeavoring to recollect the things you should do, you put an update on your calendar that tells you when you ought to do the task.

Since you are not effectively contemplating the task in the wake of setting up the update, you can give up and work on your different tasks. At the point when the date of the update comes, you get an alarm from it and play out the task at that point.

50. Turn into an early bed goer

Head to sleep early if you need to wake up the following day, early and revived.

51. Schedule your TV time

If your most loved TV show is on while you work and you feel irritated because you missed it, you might need to record it for later viewing.

Along these lines, you will work on the important assignments first and watch the show later.

52. Buy more when shopping

Whenever you are shopping, try to buy more on any one trip so you can eliminate extra trips to the store.

Specifically, when setting off to the supermarket, endeavor to design your dinners for the week, if conceivable, and purchase whatever number staple goods as could be allowed. That way, you will lessen the measure of shopping time amid that week.

53. Drink coffee carefully (2-3 mugs for each day max)

I used to be a substantial coffee consumer – 7 mugs for each day. I always felt that the more coffee I siphoned into my body, the more profitable and ready I would be.

This wasn't so. I surmise that the best container was the first of the day. The rest was the consequence of a propensity.

At last, I quit drinking excessive coffee; nowadays, it's 2-3 cups for each day. I feel that coffee doesn't benefit me in any way with regards to profitability. Or maybe, I'll drink tea (which contains significantly less caffeine than coffee and is more beneficial).

54. Kick off your evening

The following tip is a progression of tips packaged together, yet I needed to bring it up since I get such huge efficiency support while doing this.

Sooner or later, I was very worn out at work, and I had significant difficulties focusing on anything. Needless to say, my day at the workplace wasn't the most profitable.

What I did was, I got back home and took a power snooze (20 minutes). At that point, I put my running shoes on and ran a bit. I got back home, stretched my muscles, washed up, put some comfortable clothes on and ate a little bit.

It was simply unimaginable what a difference it made! It resembled being conceived again, and I was more profitable during the couple hours I worked on my business.

55. Discover your energy, transform it into your business – and complete things

Sometimes, finding your enthusiasm may not be the most straightforward thing to do but rather, when you discover it, it will help you massively in your efficiency endeavors.

The most ideal way to identify your interests is to consider the things you are great at, the things that come to you naturally, the points that you are educated about (or the ones you like to learn independently from anyone else) or the things that place you in to the "zone" (you can work hours and hours without acknowledging it).

The truth is, when you have discovered your enthusiasm and need to transform into your business, you are overly energized with the voyage ahead and inspired to put the hours in. You are not frightened of the measure of work included.

56. Have fixed working times

When we work, we typically do as such between fixed hours. When you are a business visionary, you are the manager, and you characterize your working hours.

Usually, you need to test what works best for you. For me, it is fixed timetables, since they give structure and consistency to my work.

57. Choose carefully what training you need

I used to purchase a training program in the wake of a training program (identified with web promoting). A large portion of them I never completed, nor did I actualize them. I squandered my cash and my time.

YOU CANNOT REACH SUCCESS ONLY BY WORKING HARD, YOU ALSO NEED TO BE WORKING SMART.
Charbel Tadros

I chose to change my principles when it came to training. I feel that training and learning is a critical piece of an online business person's life, yet an excessive amount is excessive – particularly if time is taken out from your center activities (those activities that you ought to focus on).

I made a standard to focus on the training that identifies with my business and focus on those courses/digital books as it were. Along these lines, I'm not investing the more significant part of my energy simply adapting, yet actualizing also.

By investigating each training course that gets discharged, I assess them very intently and endeavor to check whether they are important to my online business or not. By utilizing this criterion, I have possessed the capacity to sift through many "glossy items" which I needn't bother with.

58. Dispose of FOMO

FOMO stands for "fear of missing out." It implies that you fear missing something significant if you are not making a move on something.

An example of how this identifies with an online business is training courses. I used to purchase loads of training courses, and I was anxious about the possibility that I would pass up some vital data if I didn't buy the program.

Of course, this wasn't in this way, so I figured out how to give up and focus on the fundamental parts of my online business. I believe this is something that you likewise ought to acknowledge – new glossy stuff goes back and forth and, if you miss the pontoon, it's not the apocalypse.

59. What am I not doing now?

I need to give more credit to the book *Finding Your Focus Zone*, since I took this next tip from it.

I have utilized this inquiry to organize the different things close by. For example, I could be staring at the TV as opposed to composing a blog post, so I may ask myself, "What am I not doing now?"

This influences me to understand that I am not going to sit in front of the TV now – instead, I'll focus on composing a blog post instead of staring at the TV.

It's a straightforward inquiry – yet extremely viable.

60. Organize

We gently addressed the point of organizing in a past tip. Notwithstanding, it is vital to bring it up all alone.

When you organize, you identify the significance of your undertakings. A few assignments could compare to others, for now, so you should focus on those critical ones.

Organizing makes circumstances where you need to pick between two choices. Sometimes, the decision may not be anything but difficult to make. However, you need to consider the master plan.

For example, when I was setting up my blog, I needed to choose to surrendered briefly on perusing self-awareness books, with the goal that I had more opportunity to manufacture my blog. Although I like understanding, I can see since the choice was the correct one. Since the blog venture is presently done, I can focus on perusing once more.

61. Make a morning routine

I begin my mornings in the same way: I wake up at 05.30 AM (weekdays), get dressed, have breakfast, work 45 minutes on my blog, hit the rec center or swimming pool and after that go to the workplace.

I have found that this routine works for me. I'm ready to complete things amid the morning hours, with the goal that I have additional time toward the evening.

You may locate your ideal morning routine through trial and error. For example, you may feel that you have to eat before beginning your day or that you are better working immediately after getting out of bed. Whatever works for you is the best thing that you should stick to.

62. Make an evening routine

Your evening routine will influence your morning routine as well. A portion of the things you do in the evening is useful to your morning routine.

Doing these little things empowers you to possess more energy for the essential exercises in the morning.

63. Create workflows and processes for everything

I used to imagine that processes and workflows were the most exhausting thing ever. These days, I have changed my conclusion on this topic.

Workflows and processes enable things to go ahead easily, in a standard style. As opposed to making sense of how to accomplish something unfailingly, you have an outline to pursue. Processes and workflows empower institutionalized results on specific topics.

For instance, I have a specific workflow for distributing a blog post. At the point when this entire process is gone through, I have a blog post prepared, which gets distributed on a specific day.

It has the components of conceptualizing for a topic, composing it (without editing it), editing it (myself), editing it once more (my wife), making the last changes to the content, including pictures and recordings, distributing information about it on my rundown, planning it for a later date and after that, at long last, when the post goes alive, advancing it on social bookmarking destinations.

64. Use public support to create content

This is a tip that identifies with content advancement, and it is a decent way to create content by bringing the skill or sentiments of others into one single post.

You essentially convey an inquiry to a few people (for instance, inside your specialty) by email. At that point, you arrange the appropriate responses into one post, incorporate information about the general population in that post who took an interest to that crusade and post it to your blog.

There are numerous advantages here. You get new content onto your blog, you set up associations with others, and you bring the perspectives and aptitude of others into one single spot on a specific topic. To wrap things up, advantage is the time angle – others are essentially making the content for you; your part is generally to gather the appropriate responses into a single post and distribute it on your blog.

65. Have physical items in fixed places in your home office

To make your life simpler, as an online business visionary, you need to keep your items in fixed areas. Regardless of whether it is items that you need all the time or critical papers that you require for tax collection purposes, keep them in specific places and sorted out, with the goal that you don't sit around idly searching for them.

66. Make digital copies (bills, receipts, etc.)

Need to deal with your bills quicker? Make digital copies, if possible.

I endeavor to abstain from utilizing paper bills however much as can be expected, and I instead have my bills in electronic form. Along these lines, I don't need to invest energy dealing with paper bills.

If they are in digital form, their dealing with is a whole lot quicker, because I don't need to enter any information physically when I pay my bills utilizing an online bank. When they are in electronic form, the information is as of now filled-in, and I should favor the bill to be paid.

67. Set your bills to auto-pay

One way of taking things significantly further when the bills are concerned (along these lines of saving more opportunity to work on progressively important things) is mechanizing their installments.

Make game plans with your bank, and your bills get paid consequently on a set date.

68. Schedule your different tasks, if conceivable

You should have certain dates set for specific exercises. These may not be the most rousing tasks to deal with, yet you should do them sooner or later anyway.

69. Do small tasks now

Frequently, small tasks get postponed, because you want to deal with them later. Nonetheless, I have understood that it is smarter to get the small things (that take under 5 minutes) done immediately.

70. Work from home, if conceivable

If you are working from 9-5 and need to save time, endeavor to make working from home possible. I have done as such, and I adore it.

Mainly, I work from home on Mondays and Fridays; whatever is left of the week, I work from the office. By working from home, you save time because the driving time is removed from your daily schedule.

Although my office is essentially 5 minutes away from my home, despite everything, I save time because, when I shut down my PC, I'm as of now "back at home." This frees up my schedule for whatever remains of the night, and I possess more energy for my tasks and to assemble my online business.

CONCLUSION

Hard work and smart work are both interconnected with each other. Not everyone has the same intelligence quotient. So, they do hard work to achieve their goal. Hard work sharpens our mind and increases the accuracy to do hard things. Hard work and smart work are tightly knitted; you cannot attain the ability to do work smartly until you have done the hard work at the start. To sum up, it is to be said that hard work is the stepping stone to smart work. Hard work: trying to get answers from other ideas. Smart work: thinking and creating new ideas differently. Hard work includes penetration of the task assigned to us, and we go to depth of that thing to make sure we complete the task from start to end; it might take more time but it ensures a good job and decreases the errors, while smart work is done in a short duration to finish the task. Sometimes, it can be useful, but sometimes, it might result in disaster. We can describe smart work as a work that can be done in the right way and on the right path. In hard work, we work but without any direction, so in this way, results or success becomes uncertain.

OTHER BOOKS
WE THINK YOU WILL LOVE

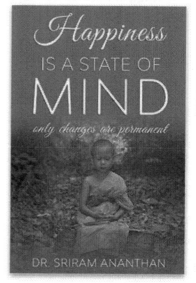

sriramananthan.com

Made in the USA
Middletown, DE
09 July 2021

43876169R00090